T0345026

THE SECOND SEEDTIME

THE SWISS LIST

Philippe Jaccottet

THE SECOND SEEDTIME

NOTEBOOKS
1980–1994

Translated by Tess Lewis

LONDON NEW YORK CALCUTTA

swiss arts council

prohelvetia

www.bibliofrance.in

This publication has
been supported by a
grant from Pro Helvetia,
Swiss Arts Council

The work is published
with the support of the
Publication Assistance
Programmes of the
Institut français

Seagull Books, 2017

Originally published in French as Philippe Jaccottet,
La Seconde Semaison
© Editions Gallimard, Paris, 1996

First published in English translation by Seagull Books, 2017
English translation © Tess Lewis, 2017

ISBN 978 0 8574 2 434 1

British Library Cataloguing-in-Publication Data
A catalogue record for this book is available from the British
Library.

Typeset by Seagull Books, Calcutta, India
Printed and bound by Maple Press, York, Pennsylvania, USA

CONTENTS

EDITORIAL NOTE

The original French edition of *The Second Seedtime* has no annotations except those few provided by Philippe Jaccottet, which appear as starred footnotes in this volume. Wherever Jaccottet's vast range of references could be traced, numbered endnotes have been added to this English translation. Unless otherwise mentioned in the notes, all translations of French and German quotations are by the volume's translator, Tess Lewis.

Semaison: The natural dispersion of a plant's seeds.

Littré

1980

JULY

Evening. Fields of lavender, in some areas the colour of slate. A large harvester advances in a cloud of dust. The fields of wheat: no longer yellow, not yet ochre. Nor gold. It is something other than a colour. The stubble.

The visible expanse extends very far, increasingly immaterial with distance, ever more sky or cloud in a slow progression—like a musical decrescendo—towards the silence of remoteness. The peace of these spaces, of these lands, of this greenery—under the blustery sky.

Walking in the thicket at eight o'clock, I raised, just two steps away, a steel-grey nightjar with wings like blades; it flew off without a cry, almost without any sound at all.

Nine fifteen. I attend the day's decantation. The sun has set. A pink band lingers above the blue-grey horizon; higher up, the sky is pale; the wind stirs, grows stronger. Is it a veil drawing back to reveal an immense, black Isis? Or is it a fading boundary, a protection guaranteed by the day against too vast a space, against the world's excessive depth? A last swallow flies past. Again a faint birdcall in the trees—and the Italian tree crickets begin to thrum: brief, stifled warning bell. The field of lavender pulls in the sky, or heralds it, begins it low to the ground. The band of light narrows, wears thin, will soon be pierced by a star or two. What has been painted one more time over the night flakes away. One voice falls silent so another less familiar, more distant voice can be heard. Once more, the cry of a jay.

The oak trees appear illuminated from within. I can make out a single distant blue mountainside through a gap in the trees. Soft bird cries persist, short trills carried away on the wind. The crickets: as if the earth itself were crackling.

Nine forty. This slow arrival of night is more of a metamorphosis, as when cloudy water in a glass clears, when its murkiness precipitates. The nightjar's rattling suddenly sets in. It's growing increasingly cool. The light sinks to the bottom of the glass like pink dust. I wait until I can drink the wine of night neat.

Nine forty-five. The invisible nightjar starts hunting. The colours fade. It's as if things were taking off their masks, their garments. The moon, almost perfectly white, the colour of wax, shines brightly at the roofline. Cold guardian of day, cold proof, a drop; or owl, immobile in the heights.

Nine fifty. First star in the east, it, too, is crackling, icy.

ε∂

Again, Masui's *Cheminements* (Wanderings): 'Soon there will no longer be a single place left on the planet where a natural life can peacefully take its course, a natural life, let us add, that is irrigated by the supernatural . . . '[1]

ε∂

Coming out of an oak forest overrun with boxwood and ivy (as by some severe thought, sombre if not funereal), a field of oats appears in the hollow of a valley: then, again, a strong emotion, a state of wonder, joy, why? I think of the encounter near Emmaus—as absurd as they appear, we must welcome these thoughts, too. It should not be only a question of colour or of the light of the bread on a table. Rather: of that which comes from elsewhere, that which returns with a particular light, slightly wan, from the world of the dead. What has passed through a screen, yet speaks to us nonetheless. Then, if I look more closely: this almost weightless multitude, sere, almost white, this ceaseless mobility, this rustling. The relation between crickets and seeds.

I continue walking west, along a path overgrown with plants (asters or dried clover) lined with old holm oak trees loaded with lichen. It's almost a precinct of wild stones in which a solemn light reigns, a cold, almost primeval light. I am astonished by the peace that emanates from these places.

AUGUST

Large yellow butterflies (swallowtails?) whose wings, seen from below, look like stained glass, chase each other over the rocks in this small area enclosed by trees, then rise in couples, higher and higher, turning white, as if they were nothing more than an intense luminous vibration or what we call flattement on flutes in early music.

But the word 'papillon' is impossible: because of the fluttering that 'papilloner' evokes, because of 'papilla', because of those two *p*'s. They should be rechristened or named according to their species when we recognize it, if that doesn't come off as overly erudite. They're like things *detached* from a whole, like fragments—a little bit like ashes; because they seem to float at random, letting themselves be carried, hesitant. The nightjar, who feeds on them, fumbles around as they do when night falls.

Auriga, the Charioteer, like a house drawn in chalk by a child.

In Petrarch's sonnets, which I'm rereading, the (internal) inflection is only momentarily audible within an occasionally artificial construction, a line of reasoning, a rhetoric, which it illuminates retrospectively.

Shortly before five o'clock in the morning: under a moon reduced by half, Aldebaran, enormous above the trees. A cool wind rises—after a suffocating day and night. The crickets persevere, tireless.

Before long, I correct myself: 'Aldebaran, enormous' is Venus. The wind seems to reach us from the depths of nocturnal space. A shooting star passes. At five thirty, the constellations continue to rise, the sky turns silver along the horizon, a nearby house is vaguely illuminated.

A quarter of an hour later, only Venus and the moon are still visible. The wind, now softer, blows at the oak trees in short gusts. No more crickets.

At six o'clock, a first bird cry, timid, like the creak of a hinge, hoarse.

Is dawn the inverse of night? Not at all. No more than gold is the inverse of silver. The landscape emerges from limbo; and it is still, or is almost, cold. Wheat and lavender: night and morning.

It's not yet seven o'clock. I climb onto the rocks; the sky is clear: a nightjar flies up in front of me. The mountains to the east are a slate-coloured mist, the grasses white as fits the hour.

Madrigal by Gesualdo (*Moro, lasso* . . .): as if cries and laments were rising from the stars themselves, as if the star-filled night were coming to life, were sounding its voice—in a polyphony resembling the distances between the stars. Purification of the cry.

The Plaint in Purcell's *Fairy Queen*. Deller's voice is like one who travels abroad and returns to his homeland—or simply leaves home and returns. His voice has a hearth—or roots. Just as a bird's flight is not absolutely free but obeys invisible laws.

Oriole: bird linked to the eight o'clock morning sun, to the still-elongated shadows in the orchards, the truffle groves.

Clouds, almost completely white, racing across the sky above the trees, in the scintillation of the greenery and the radiance, the white fire of the August sky— with the mistral; they dissipate almost instantaneously, like smoke, and are absorbed by the light. Like stains erased by summer's intensity, like words resorbed by a sovereign silence. This is, perhaps, a way to approach that 'joy', whose name I traced one day when contemplating how removed and nearly incomprehensible it had become for us. The entire landscape is like a fire fanned by an almost cool wind, a fire of light, of refulgence—and, in another way, of water. The four elements joined together, not to say muddled in our confused and deep apprehension. Everything is brought to incandescence by the air, yet without scorching us. And so we can consider the buzzard's wondrous flight to be one of the world's emanations, leaves torn from the earth that play as they rise. Their pale, speckled plumage, why so beautiful?

Grasshoppers, sparks bursting from the flaming ground; arid earth already beginning to crack in places. Grasses the colour of straw, slight, arched, supple, versatile—in the intense heat that heightens the power of all things.

The buzzard passes, rapidly, in the blinding light.

In the east, Orion is quickly wiped away by the day's fire, burnt by it, like a ladder.

At night, the moment the moon rises, orange, still almost full, amid the clouds and the black trees, a shooting star falls vertically. It seems, in falling, to burrow into the silence.

We randomly follow very narrow paths, barely visible on the hillside. The last flowers, yellow blossoms, whose names I've never learnt. Suddenly, the large rocks that protrude amid the grass between the trees look like altar tables adorned by a dragonfly's twitching flight.

I feel scattered, dismantled; sometimes the images I seize upon are as well. They disperse in the fiery air, in summer's hot, carnal light. As if they've divined my disarray, they refuse to ripen. I'm not worthy of them. The fire that stirs dully in my core is not one that can nourish them. Summer whispers its counsel, burning, desperate, or too late, to the body. The rose-bay speaks through as many cool as burning mouths.

Barefoot in the warm dirt. Clumps that crumble in hand. Ploughed earth. Its colour here, in spots, is the shade of warm brick with tones from yellow to red: colours that are dense, thick; but in the earth they are as calm as blue and green are elsewhere, and more stable. It's the ground, the sedimentary rock. Paths, also the colour of brick or fire between the stalks of grass, the prairies. Some grasses are extremely tenuous, sparse, almost weightless, nothing more than a trembling of heat. Vibrant earth.

(We are lame: shackled, wounded, not allowed to run, much less fly.)

Dog rose blooming on your garland
arc (with which Petrarch could have adorned Laura)
pure garland hung here and there in the fields
for beauty absent or destroyed
weightless—open and pure

childlike flower
crown for her who has left our world
who today no longer sits among the
white or pink
native grasses

or arch under which we pass anywhere, bowing
slightly
wild and indigent
door left ajar . . .

Flowers lit by day like constellations of embers
pink council
flowers with barely a hint of red

The viper lives, invisible, among these rocks
silent, swift.

Enormous clouds loaded with rain
like mountains or shades
or fruits ripening, ready to burst.

Divided, but present; filled with doubts but still more
genuinely here, in the moment, not in the past or in

the future. Having welcomed for days the light in its diversity and variations, from the silver of dawn to the gold of twilight; rising to receive its reflections multiplied in the celestial dust beyond sight.

The light of the day's end dissipates like a fragrance.

SEPTEMBER

The nightjars have already gone: fleeting companions. Punctual heralds of twilight with their wooden clock sound. Heralds of the in-between, between earth and sky, between day and night—skimming the tops of the trees.

A decantation occurs at the same time as the day darkens bit by bit—and that's when this bird the colour of shadow appears, rather peaceful, floating, around which I revolve more or less in vain. Like a swatch of night cut from its cloth.

When the brilliant smoke of the day dissipates.

Among the most delicate grasses, the fescue.

Folgóre di San Gimignano's poems of the week and of the months, late thirteenth, early fourteenth century, have the same elegant splendour, vivid and joyful, as many Renaissance paintings; particularly the smaller works: predellas or cassone decorations. Pleasure and refinement.

Under the sun's banner, its fiery pavilion; already a bit whiter, perhaps.

A luminous column, the sky atop this column. Jubilant insects.

Between five and six in the evening, shadows lengthen over yellower fields, the distances become clearer in barely gilded dust, those are almost boats or islands on the horizon.

A feeling of benediction and grace. Voices carry far without becoming intelligible. Happy are those who could, without dishonesty or indifference, bind a prayer to these moments of the day.

The snow's light in the rooms. I think of the verses in Leopardi's *Ricordanʒe*:

> In queste sale antiche,
> Al chiaror delle nevi . . .

Perhaps we live in a desert, in a night that may not have night's beauty. A sense of deterioration that seems widespread wears us down in turn. When someone says, 'God is dead,' it doesn't in the slightest sound like an exclamation of joy. And yet, something strange: I hear these few words in Italian about the snow (and on other days it will be other words) like a sound of silver—much as, it seems to me, the devout must hear the bells of the Elevation. Almost exactly the same way. At this point of intersection, once more: the other world. Ours?

1981

Between two pages of work, in the middle of the afternoon, I go out. The Montagne de la Lance seems flecked with snow down to its base; I think of the Tibetan music I've been listening to over the past few days which is made to resound very loudly against tremendous mountains. The monks' voices are extremely low and strong and seem to ruminate the sounds, voices of oxen harnessed to plough slowly, obstinately, the field of eternity. The instruments sometimes evoke enormous gusts of wind or lashes of a whip that make you flinch, domesticated and deprived of the spaces for which this music is made as you are.

Once again, I wonder about the significance of the fact that I find it so beautiful and powerful, like certain pages of the Old Testament.

I read somewhere that a Hilton was going to be built in Lhasa. And so the highest sacred place on earth will be destroyed to a certain extent, though it has already been broached by the existence of those recordings, of photographs, of increasingly indiscreet reportage. (But weren't these intrusions possible precisely because it had already been destroyed?) How should one conduct oneself with regard to this ruin occurring at an ever-faster pace and which Leopardi presented as desperate more than a hundred years ago?

These men with shaven heads who could have conquered the world on their galloping horses or amassed a fortune trading rare goods, were they right to speak that way to divinities as implacable and radiant as the mountains?

Milarepa. I'm thinking of him because of the Tibetan music I've discovered these days. This book, which several of my friends admire, left me almost completely cold, except for a few pages. Why? Is it frivolous to ask what the point of these ascetic exploits is? This, certainly, is far from the yoga that is in fashion, and so much the better; but to retreat from the world and eat only nettles to the point where one takes on their colouring in order to escape the laws of the body, is that not lunacy?

The awareness that I'm trampling these questions becomes more and more paralysing—because year after year I'm thrown back on the same contradiction without having made the slightest progress, or, rather, with some regression: the sinking of the scales' negative pan. Clarity recedes, becomes scarce, night approaches and solidifies as the heart shrivels. And it seems I know in advance that nothing I read (of the most profound philosophers or greatest saints) will penetrate deep enough to change me. Hence these books opened, paged through, soon closed again, too soon surely—unless they are books of poetry, still able to enlighten me for a time, for a certain distance—like glimpses of nature. And it's possible that these glimpses grow so faint, so rare, that even the words to express them no longer crystallize.

'Such an image, still, perhaps . . . ': these words came to me in half-sleep—without continuing. Thus I felt like someone whose hand starts trembling more and more when building a house of cards that seemed at one time almost inhabitable. And in the silence I am trying to recreate within, as I did at the time of *L'Ignorant* (The Ignorant One), having become even more ignorant, it hardly seems possible that one word or another will come to me again; in my inner impoverishment.

How can one imagine or hope—once the day's colours have finally been erased, drawn out, and increasingly resemble silver, a veil slowly worn down to the weft before night—that eyes destroyed might open again onto black depths in which luminous figures might appear, figures different from those in familiar constellations and in a different space?

These doors that seem to open, the images, etc.

Like a hand placed on a shoulder
that gives a gentle push to the timorous,
the light of the snow on the crest,
    barely . . .

After several such 'encounters' and a pretence of thought (insufficient, of course, and what was it that inhibited me?), after many years now, having been able to ascertain only one thing, always the same:

    'as if a door were opening . . . '

Like the dog rose, which surprised me each time I saw it. Its branches formed an arch under which one was tempted to pass, as if to enter a different space while nonetheless aware that it was, in a sense, not 'real'.

Like the invisible stream beneath the abundant, thorny, impenetrable bushes—its voice, eternal, elusive, seeming to come, it, too, from somewhere else within the 'here',

and all poetry of this order, all music, all painting,

converging towards what is secret and without name.

The end of a dream: on a staircase around the lift's grated cage, cards have been placed as if for a five or six-person game of lotto, along with stacks of chips or wads of notes, I can't remember. I see myself playing alone with a young woman (the other players are in the flat, although still taking part in the game, perhaps through my intermediary). She is very likely imaginary, yet a cheerful brunette of the southern type. We laugh a great deal while playing, over nothing, and sometimes our hands or knees brush fleetingly and unintentionally. Brief moments of happiness.

On the radio, a *Miserere* attributed to Pergolesi. The word 'volute' occurs to me, as does its relation to the word 'voluptuous'. This music with its Neapolitan spirit and melodies that are perhaps too facile but are constant, inexhaustible, is first and foremost the ear's pleasure and is very near the Baroque, much nearer, it seems to me, than Bach's music. It's truly the joy of swirling, flowing, flying; it's a tender and not very deep jubilation in which the angels are so many little cherubs and the saints so many swooning women. It is, literally, exuberance that I find neither in Bach nor in Mozart. They ascend higher, on other paths.

FEBRUARY

The almond, a kind of seashell made from wood dotted with pores.

The sentence from *The Conference of the Birds* seen in Paris in Peter Brook's moving production (the birds have come to the Valley of Annihilation, but an astrologer gives them a bit of courage to go beyond it): 'Even if the two worlds were suddenly annihilated, one should not deny the existence of a single grain of sand from the earth. If there were not a single trace left of men or of saints, pay attention to the secret in a drop of rain.'[2] That could serve as an epigraph for all the books of poetry one might still dare to write and publish today.

There is an analogy between my remote rejection of surrealism and that of the mystical. It was motivated by the desire to illuminate a middle way: that may have been too lazy a dream.

These days I sometimes understand more clearly, or with more nostalgia, those visionaries for whom light is a dazzlement beyond doubt and not something close to a lure. On the low road, one risks losing all clarity. Perhaps that path is fundamentally more difficult?

If one has no other guide than the minute reflection of pink on the torn edge of an angel's wing, what help is that? When a conflagration would be necessary for scaling the wall. Or is all this once again nothing more than words that enchant and have little power over everyday reality?

Too removed from beings? like a fugitive hiding in the light, in dawn.

Like a fugitive hidden in the light of dawn . . .

MARCH

Work in the garden, in fine weather, under a pale sky. No new leaves except for the tiny ones of the spiraea. The robin, Emily Dickinson's 'the one in Red Cravat' so dear to Roud in his old age, seems to accompany my work or even take an interest in it, he is so close;

more a pedestrian than a bird, almost always busy pecking at the ground.

Parisian dream. We are waiting in a queue to enter the theatre. The box office seems to be at the top of a narrow staircase crowded with people speaking energetically; the line is not moving and, impatient, I decide to climb the stairs. As I do so, I jostle very young dancers in costume, which is not disagreeable. I finally reach a small room on the same floor as the box office and have a heated argument with the ticket-clerk, a man of a certain age, insignificant. I explain to him that I am with several elderly people, among them, my nonagenarian mother. I get my way. Then I notice a relatively young man sitting on a chair against the wall and giving me a vague smile. I realize I have met him but cannot recall his name, which embarrasses me; probably a writer I had met once at Gallimard.

After the show (forgotten), I see him walking off with a girlfriend. We greet each other; we're in a very large square on an incline that evokes one of those vacant lots created by bombing raids during the war. From that point on, anxiety suffuses the scenes like water. It's very late, I understand that this theatre is very much off the beaten path, there aren't any taxis, the roads are badly lit, the passers-by shady. In front of a facade, harshly illuminated, groups of dubious young people are loitering. I assume it's a porn theatre or a seedy music hall. They appear very aggressive. I'm carrying a briefcase I don't want to lose at any price. Further on, where things become ever darker, even sinister, there are people who seem to be waiting for a train. Panic overtakes me. I wake the moment a toad-like dwarf attacks my legs, completely grey in the grey darkness of this miserable neighbourhood.

APRIL

Hopkins has fascinated me for a long time (since Leyris' first translations were published in 1957) as has Hölderlin, though the latter with less distance since I could read him in the original. I saw Hopkins ascend just as high in the poetic air and fall back to earth no less painfully. But with a much greater attention to and knowledge of the visible—which is perhaps natural when you move from Germany to England (although Goethe contradicts me on this point).

> My aspens dear, whose airy cages quelled,
> Quelled or quenched in leaves the leaping
> sun . . . [3]

These few words are almost nothing (and are, moreover, in translation but a reflection); and yet they're enough for me to be immediately struck, to be taken once more in my lifetime, beyond all thought and doubt, by the power of poetry. When, once again, I was about to ask myself why and no doubt wouldn't have arrived at any explanation if I had.

In 'Moonrise':

> The moon, dwindled and thinned to the fringe
> of a finger-nail held to the candle . . . [4]

We would not have been alone in seeing this, in being surprised and touched as if by the pealing of a small bell reaching us from a distant mountain temple.

Later, 'that blue is all in a rush / With richness';[5] these traces of Eden, the intensity of the thrush's song, as I just noted the song of the warbler in the linden tree. I have the feeling I'm in a relay race, from poet to poet, regardless of the difference in levels; but also a feeling of trampling.

In 'The Lantern Out of Doors', those who pass by like lanterns disappearing in the night with Christ as their only recourse.

The long June evenings behind the village of Bayonne. After nine o'clock, it's still hot; not a breath of wind, a few light clouds turn pink. The immobility, the silence, and the beauty of the landscape render it almost unreal, incomprehensible. A few nightingales sing here and there, but briefly. Pale greens, yellowing greens, the lavender's first blue, a simple veil covering the plants, the mountain's blue, the weak blue of the sky. The fields, in these combes, like water that would wed them, flowing down towards Grignan.

The sound of water in the gardens of Foulon, from place to place, light and clear, almost cold under the half-moon.

This morning, with a light north wind, the mountains once again are as limpid as water—as joy?

The field of wheat (or barley) luminous at night, around ten o'clock—the cherry tree laden with fruit of an intense red, beyond this blade—and the moon almost full. This light of the wheat field in the peaceful night—and a few sheep under the oak trees. A night-jar, distant.

JULY

Dream. A large house that recalls a prison more than a residence in the midst of a move, half-empty; we are nevertheless captives, a crowd of us. Some come to meet us, eyes beaten, their faces neither terrified nor injured, but marked by some indistinct deformation; we know that these are the ones who are 'returning'. Later, we are grouped in enormous rooms, waiting. When a door opens, we have to hide wherever we can, behind trunks, for example, because it's always possible that someone will shoot. On the other side of the room I see someone grabbing A.M.'s watch after having done this to others and I see that A.M. is being hurt. Then the man (an ordinary man, without a uniform) comes up to me (unless it's a different man), checks his notebook in which he sees, with malicious glee, that something has been written down (I also see the page and the initials). It has to do with the fact that I have a ball made of the extremely hard rubber that lets it bounce almost indefinitely (a toy that was the fashion for a time and with which my son was playing here just yesterday)—this seems, in the eyes of the 'guard' to be an infraction equal to the illegal possession of a weapon. In any case, for me, it's an aggravating circumstance; hence my worry. And I see myself, I hear myself saying, pleading, putting all my hope into a few words as he leaves the room: 'Do you have children?', implying: 'With whom you might have played as I did with my son?' And I understand immediately from his silence that he doesn't have any—that there is, therefore, no hope. All the prisoners in the dream were badly dressed with the tired and sullen expressions you often see in crowds in the East.

This is what fills our nights, what they can be made of. Woken around five thirty by the prolonged sound of a peculiar siren—announcing, as it were, a cosmic accident.

The warbler in the linden tree: an extraordinarily, mysteriously clear song, as if it were crossing, piercing an envelope, passing a limit.

Connection with what I'm reading of Suhrawardi's, whose images, especially in the beautiful story 'The Purple Archangel' resemble the ignorant's errant intuitions.

Or even actual encounters like yesterday afternoon, the two little hoopoes in the dust on the path, their heads like light hammers. In Suhrawardi, they are guides of mystic navigation:

But at night we climbed up to the castle that presided over the immensity of space and we looked in through one of its windows. Doves often came to us from the forests of Yemen and informed us how things were in that forbidden region. Sometimes a bright light from Yemen came to us, its bright flash from the 'right side', from the 'oriental' side, told us about the families living in the Najd. A breeze filled with the aromatic scent of the arak awakened in us transports of ecstasy. Then we sighed with desire and nostalgia for our homeland.

And so we climbed up at night and came back down during the day. Then, one night when the moon was full, we saw a hoopoe come through the window and greet us. In its beak it held a message 'from a blessed spot on the right side of the valley, from inside a bush'.

It said to us: 'I have seen the method of your delivery and bring both of you "truthful news from the Kingdom of Sheba". All is explained in this message from your father.'

I find it touching that the 'star of Yemen' that shines in this text is Canopus because I have loved this star since I discovered it one day this summer shortly before dawn.

Field of wheat in the afternoon. It's like pale gold, like metal, a *blade*—at the same time it's straw, it's dust: How to find the *mots justes*? Under the oak trees or in their clearings, their movable ramparts, shadowy, half-nocturnal.

Solar straw. Their spikes, their upright beards; rods of brass? Rather it is both colour and matter, sometimes closer to silver than gold; a quivering, too, as if shadows were passing over them, or flights of birds? I don't know what it is: profound, elementary, secret.

A scorching blade?

Virginia Woolf, near the end of *Orlando*:

> What has praise and fame to do with poetry? What has seven editions (the book had already gone into no less) got to do with the value of it? Was not writing poetry a secret transaction, a voice answering a voice? So that all this chatter and praise and blame and meeting people who admired one and meeting people who did not admire one was

as ill suited as could be to the thing itself—a voice answering a voice. What could have been more secret, she thought, more slow, and like the intercourse of lovers, than the stammering answer she had made all these years to the old crooning song of the woods, and the farms and the brown horses standing at the gate, neck to neck, and the smithy and the kitchen and the fields, so laboriously bearing wheat, turnips, grass, and the garden blowing irises and fritillaries?[6]

The cicada works like a carpenter. We are almost tempted to look for the sawdust left by its song. Its voice is stronger than any other; the voice of the luminous present. Suited to the stalks, to the stubble.

'Oh David! I am finished with homes. I live with those whose hearts are broken.' It's an enigmatic phrase in Suhrawardi's treatise *The Language of the Ants*. I am perhaps not hearing it properly, but it resonates deep within me.

Like this one, from Attar's *Book of Affliction*: 'Who knows how far a humble old woman's prayers at dawn are able to reach?'

The day's radiance—the crest of the mountain is visible again between the trees because some were cut down —the day's almost immobile radiance—summer: its sparks, the crack of planks—and the gusting wind, as hard as stone.

A sudden storm, violent, brief. Swifts seem to shoot out from it forcefully, one after another, flying as fast as their wings can take them, sometimes seeming to oscillate from their haste. To the east, the sky has whitish, ghostly patches, other patches are black; in the west, the sky above the hills is the colour of sulphur with gashes of grey.

Nine o'clock at night. Clouds that have come from the northwest, the colour of mountain snowstorms, cold, iron grey, aggressive—like menacing smoke, with barely a hint of pink from the setting sun. Short, passing rain showers on the leaves. Like an icy hand, a cold blade slashing the air. Shades of pewter, of silver, of iron. As if emerging from a demonic mouth, from a sepulchre. It is blowing from a place of death. Under the razing beams of sun, the plain is violet and dark green. Closer, some of the pine tree trunks seem to be ablaze. Thorny rain.

Around three in the afternoon, the telephone rings. I hear something like a man's grunting or grumbling; then silence. This is not a dream. A joke in bad taste? A plea? I'll never know.

In the morning, there's already that light that takes me back every year, without fail, to a long-ago crossing of Lake Neuchâtel in a small boat towards Estavayer, at a time when the town looked to me like a small Swabian city, the kind Hölderlin must have seen before he invoked the 'philosophical light' around his window that, a century and a half later, would fascinate Roud as the drafts of his *Requiem* attest, drafts which should be published some day.

AUGUST

Corbin's book on Ibn Arabi culminates with a comparison of 'theophany' and 'incarnation'. There is the way of 'sacred purity' and the one that includes suffering, the child Christ and the adult Christ facing each other on the walls of Sant' Apollinare Nuovo in Ravenna; in my day-dreaming, I sometimes brushed on this confrontation of eternity and time.

The extraordinary degradation in the use of the words 'seraphim' and especially 'cherubim', the first two orders of angels: all you need to measure the decline is to reread Canto XXVIII of the *Paradiso*, verses 100–02:

> Cosi veloci seguono i suoi vimi,
> per somigliarsi al punto quanto ponno;
> e posson quanto a veder son sublimi.

> Thus swiftly their own bonds do they pursue
> to grow as like the one point as they may;
> the which they may, the more their vision is
> true.[7]

Walking along paths that are almost completely erased and will be lost; in some sections it's like walking on embers that do not burn. With only butterflies for company in the sunny sections.

Walking. The paths speak, or come close to doing so, when they are disappearing.

We saw Pierre-Albert Jourdan yesterday. A simu-
lacrum of a little old man. Fidgety, but still himself,
even if just a shadow of his former self; maintaining
his sense of humour, his curiosity in things, showing
us an English book on Cézanne's late paintings, won-
dering where he could find a good one on Rembrandt.
I don't believe he is feigning; what he has suffered has,
therefore, not destroyed him.

Dream. A young man (the intense, skinny type of cer-
tain agile and incisive intellectuals) forces me to shoot
a bow and arrow at someone (I no longer have any
idea who it was or if I had known at the time, probably
also a young man). I look with alarm at the tip of the
arrow, sharp enough to kill. Because I miss, no doubt
on purpose, he makes me repeat the ordeal. I try to
escape his hold; I have to shoot in a kind of gallery or
underground passage that is full of people. I point out
to him that one of the arrows is bent, trying my best
to evade him. He specifies that if a group of young
Israelis cycle past at the moment I shoot the arrow, it
won't make any difference because in any case they
are Romans. I object, incensed by this old theory
meant to justify anti-Semitism. I insult him, our argu-
ment turns very violent. I finally shout that I won't

shoot unless it's at him. I try to run away (at this point we are on Place Saint François in Lausanne). At a certain point he says to me, still extremely aggressive and coercive, 'Does she like stamps?' Then he goes and buys some. 'She' is my daughter. I realize he wants to kill her with poison on the stamps' glue. I protest. Finally, I get away from him.

This man was, literally, the devil. The atmosphere of the dream was one of violence, extreme evil and brutal conflict.

Morning sun on the stones, wood worn by the weather, a mildness that is difficult to express—especially since the air is almost immobile, the movement of the leaves silent—like a child moving his hand while dreaming. The oleander is still in bloom, has been for weeks now—so mysterious although we seldom think of them as such. Why was it necessary to have flowers—or colours? Their pink—matchless: a coolness. Or like when children carry lit lanterns for celebrations. Lanterns in broad daylight. But also as a flowering of the earth, a metamorphosis, the coins, the seeds' small coins. The force they conceal that makes them split, makes them emit a fragile shoot, etc.

The soul's seed? Us in the maternal body.

Flowers to cross the river of the underworld, seeds or obolos.

The spirit would like to use like a lantern the one who steers boats on rivers at night.

'You have boarded . . . '

Like the one who lights a lantern on his prow if he ventures at night in channels between the reeds,

take this flower to light your passage through the day . . .

Even daylight, even the most vivid light, even a very mild September are not easy to cross . . .

The fact that we can't say any old nonsense is something I find very mysterious and very comforting.

This morning, just when I'm getting out of bed (it's not quite eight and there's a chill), I hear someone's voice from the floor below; it's A. and I wonder why he has come back since we said goodbye last night and he was meant to leave very early for Geneva. F. follows him; because I hear the word 'dead', I immediately think of my little nephew, who is ill. But it's Pierre-Albert Jourdan, whose wife had tried unsuccessfully to reach us last night. He died early Sunday morning of an aortic rupture. The night before he had asked that the curtains be drawn so the light wouldn't wake him. He called for help around five in the morning; his wife said that he had time to see his death and then everything went very quickly. As grief-stricken as she is, she thinks, as do we, that this death has spared her the worst; the week after our visit had been a bad one, despite the interruption of his radiation treatment. Things could only have got worse.

Outside, a light mistral along with the golden light and deep shadows of evening, which his absence neither increases nor lessens. For us his absence will always be very palpable.

Folds in the distance, hollowed out by the setting sun's pure light. That he is deprived of this . . . Or not? Infinite question.

The next day, sunrise at seven o'clock. Around seven thirty, the Ventoux turned pink behind hills that were still blue; thus the rising sun excavates the distances, separates the mountain ranges as the sky turns a brilliant shade of pale yellow; the sun is just touching the first treetops; and a window. The second dawn Jourdan could not see . . .

Last night the sunset created a mythic sky. In the past, we might have said the sky was celebrating that soul's arrival. To the south, large rising bands of very pink clouds are separated by bands of intensely blue sky, like flowers; and to the east, just above the horizon, a strange cloud of an orange pink colour, an almost raw shade, in the shape of a bird or a butterfly covered in brass scales.

Funeral. A light of extreme limpidity and strength; no wind; the sky an intense blue; the view very clear in the distance. Between Beaumes-de-Venise and Caromb, I think of Tuscany. The market is set up in the square, behind the church which I enter to ask about the time of the service; a large woman gracing the altar draws my attention to the first ringing of bells, a descending motif, a slow cascade of notes that continues as I go back out into the bright sun. Further on, colourful trestle tables are set up for a village festival. When we arrive at La Gardette, we're delighted to see Paul de R. Next to him, a figure of great delicacy, leaning forward slightly, not without some resemblance to Yves Bonnefoy, and whom I later recognize as Alain L. They arrived from Paris in the night with another of Pierre-Albert's friends, François L., a young, bearded redhead. Damien greets us, eyes red, then Fabienne, pale and gracious, all in black. We enter. The coffin has just been sealed—in place of the table where we had tea yesterday. This polished object with its heavy metalwork seems as foreign to the world of the person it is now intended to receive as it could possibly be.

In tears, S. evokes the awful week she has just passed, her fear of suffering. Concerned about possible attacks, they'd had to buy a gun. The thought of his wanting to commit suicide must have immediately occurred to them, just as it does to us now, because they bought the heaviest and most cumbersome model they could, for fear of actually using it. Little Mrs J., his mother, is there too, sitting in an armchair, sunk in grief. We return to the car. On the square, people from the village, relatives, René Char standing to one side, leaning against a low wall—tall, a black scarf around his neck, a cane in hand. Anne stands next to him. He will stay outside.

The funeral service, in French, without a note of music, without any mention of Pierre-Albert's books is revoltingly banal, amplified by a noisy microphone that no one thinks of unplugging or is able to shut off. We tell each other that it would have made Pierre-Albert smile and that one moment, perhaps, would have touched him: when the censer, that Tibetan object, was swung in front of his coffin. Not a single moment of emotion. Obviously Pierre-Albert is not here—he's already dispersed into the light.

We walk down to the cemetery with René Char and Anne; large, beautiful pine trees line the road. Thin steles of pale yellow limestone, unusually elegant, stand near the grave. I feel strangely absent. The sky's radiance is impudent.

OCTOBER

October Dawn

The air is a bit colder

The redstart sings in the dissipating dawn

It's as if a piece of coal were singing.

DECEMBER

Pull back this curtain of snow . . .

1982

The stream: an advancing murmur, escorted by that of the trees, of the birds hidden along its edges.

Hopkins again.

A little more than a hundred years ago, on 28 September 1881, Hopkins, having deployed all the complexity of his art to paint the landscape with the 'darksome burn' of Inversnaid, expresses the wish that is, in contrast, very simple:

> What would the world be, once bereft
> Of wet and wildness? Let them be left,
> O let them be left, wildness and wet;
> Long live the weeds and the wilderness yet.[8]

Farther on, in 'The Blessed Virgin Compared to the Air We Breathe', he questions the air, the sky, that 'will not stain light' but will protect us from blindness, like the Virgin makes God 'sweeter'.

From a sorrowful sonnet of 1885:

> Natural heart's ivy, Patience masks
> Our ruins of wrecked past purpose
> [. . .]
> And where is he who more and more distils
> Delicious kindness?—He is patient. Patience
>   fills
> His crisp combs, and that comes those ways
>   we know.[9]

FEBRUARY

Moon veiled or crowned with haze. The same haze trails like scarves over the meadows, the gardens (at six in the evening, while the day's clarity lasts). This brings the heavenly body closer, turns it into a kind of flower.

That phrase of Villiers de l'Isle-Adam quoted by Mallarmé—'Living? Our servants will do that for us'—characterizes in its very excess, the temptation of that era, its aspects of grandeur and its risk of aberration.

In any case, I note, on rereading Mallarmé—while the birds outside imagine it is April—that his power endures (in part, no doubt to his nobility of soul, to his spirit's tension without complacency), even if I sense in it a lack of air; a rarefaction of the air with the cold glittering of the constellations, which he had tried to make his poems to equal.

February moon. The thousands of rosemary blossoms are the colour of the sky after sunset, whereas the moon's splendour grows brighter—and the last birds give faint cries.

Express this grace. Carried above the mists or smoke into the open church of the sky. A raised host? without being exalted by any priest. This suspended mist (or smoke) like silence made visible: trails of silence, of near absence, of unreality.

I welcomed you, robins—or converging streams—in the bare tree and thin, clear light above my hands.

The earth smells of smoke.

Whistler, in his 'Ten O'Clock Lecture' of 1888, translated by Mallarmé:

> The people have been harassed with Art in every guise, and vexed with many methods as to its endurance . . .
>
> And so, for the flock, little hamlets grow near Hammersmith, and the steam horse is scorned.[10]

In the fig tree's almost white, almost brilliant branches (a bright, gay shade of ash, shimmer of pre-spring light); in this pellucid frame, the robin's song is even more limpid.

When the day is like water. The sun itself, prudent like water.

Few clouds, weightless, white as well. Sparse, luminous, accentuating instead of veiling the light. Careless. As if they were the traces, in broad daylight, of fireworks or of a bouquet thrown high into the sky.

The woods are of branching light.

Perhaps one of the things that alienates me from the Mallarmean dream is its taste for theatre, even though

I understand and even share it when, coming upon a fairground spectacle, he made of it a cosmic vision. I recognize very well that 'in my domain' I can forgo all 'scenes', that this is another matter altogether. Is it due to his disdain or fear of the natural, of nature, etc.? Inherited from Baudelaire?

'The White Water Lily'. There's a model text, twenty years before the 'Faun' in which Mallarmé's musings revolve in summer's torpor around one of his centres with a cheerful nonchalance: 'the dispersed virginal absence' or the 'feminine possibility', which his realization might well destroy, beautifully rendered by 'one of those magical, closed water lilies ... enveloping nothingness in their hollow whiteness, made of intact dreams, of happiness that will never come ... ', compared again, later, to 'a noble swan's egg, from which no flight will ever burst.' This is Mallarmé turning to his centre and wresting a marvel from nothingness with unsurpassable subtlety and precision—as when he writes about the autumn forest in 'Glory': 'towards the ecstatic torpor of the leaves beyond, too immobilized not to be scattered in the air by some gust'. A perfection of phrasing that astounds me, but also seems to *imprison* me by depriving me of a more natural breath, which is indispensable to my endorsement. (Besides, Mallarmé himself liked to compare a book to a casket; casket or vial, soon: tomb.)

Little by Mallarmé touches me more than what he wrote about Hamlet, 'the adolescent who vanished from us at the beginning of life' (and that barbed phrase later in the text: 'the fateful prince who will perish with his first step into manhood melancholically pushes from his blocked path with the useless point of his sword the load of loquacious emptiness he would risk becoming in turn had he grown older'); Hamlet, or the poet 'reading the book of himself'; because he is reflected in this character with such melancholy and such purity.

As in every passage in which he imagines his highest utopia and affirms his poetry's excellence: 'a book, in our hands, if it expresses some august idea, replaces all theatres, not by making us forget them, but on the contrary by recalling them imperiously. The metaphorical sky that spreads around the lightning flash of the verse, artifice par excellence, to the point of simulating little by little and incarnating the heroes (only what we must perceive so that we are bothered by their presence, a trait): this background of ecstasy, spiritually and magnificently illuminated, is certainly the purity we carry within, always ready to burst out on occasions that are always lacking in existence or outside of art.' There is something admirable, which continues to fascinate; but . . . how to justify this 'but'? This lightning and this sky have lost a bit too much, in passing, of their inherent power just as the Woman of another time, 'primeval and naïve', in 'Future Phenomenon' has become decidedly too remote. Perhaps lightning and sky in Mallarmé have suffered for being closed up in rue de Rome among too many 'abolished trinkets'? It's when one notices this that one rushes back to Rimbaud the Savage or Verlaine the Disconcerted to catch one's breath.

. . . To the nascent, miraculous blue of February evenings. To this wing? to this flight? because there is a softening, an opening, an extension of the light—but it is still barely perceptible: a beginning, a start, grace. Pigeon. Slate. We push the night away a bit more—we extend the roof of light, we stand beneath its unfolding wing. (This is what can be formulated in thought from a distance; in the moment, you experience it differently—and that's what counts most. We feel what those children feel who refuse to go home, who prolong their games, shouting happily. We feel the day advancing on obscurity with an infinite gentleness that moves us to tears.)

Mallarmé is one of the first to have written (admirable) poetry about poetry: 'the inkwell, crystalline as consciousness, with its drop, at the bottom, of shadows relative to having something exist: then, take away the lamp.' Yet he has had a formidable posterity in the diluted and sterile reworkings of his obsessions. Bloodless Narcissus.

He dreamt of the 'hymn' ('harmony and joy') as Hölderlin had almost a century earlier. However, solitary and refined as he was, he couldn't hope to achieve even a fragment of it.

MARCH

Octogenarian Michaux, in *Corner Posts*:

> Keep your weakness intact.

> If you follow a route, be careful, you'll have trouble returning to the openness.

> There is still limpidity in you.

And echoing Blake's tiger:

> Lord tiger, it's a trumpet blast through his whole being when he spots his prey; it's a sport, a chase, an adventure, a climb, a destiny, a liberation, a fire, a light.
>
> Whipped by hunger, he leaps.

Who dares compare his seconds to those?

Who has had even ten tiger seconds in his entire life?

Later:

Music, long close to poetry.

A reed flute was enough. When the breath approaches and passes through it, nostalgia comes out. 'Its nostalgia, which man immediately recognized as his own—even though its nostalgia is more graceful—and it enchanted him, whether shepherd, or passer-by, or princess. Space created it and it created space in turn.'[11]

JULY

Whoever is curious about Goethe and the circumstances of a poem's creation must read the account he wrote in old age in the appendix of *Campaign in France* of his 1777 winter journey in the Harz Mountains, a journey that inspired the famous poem of the same name (the poem through which Rilke said he first recognized Goethe's greatness). The strange story of the young Plessing, whose unhappy fate, in contrast to that of the poet favoured by fortune, becomes the poem's hearth around which are ordered 'things seen' in the mountains. Goethe, having received Plessing's distressed confidences, had remained silent but decided to visit him at the end of his journey; which he did without being recognized by Plessing, who then complained at length about Goethe's lack of response, upon which the latter, disguised as a member of the court of Weimar, lavished therapeutic advice on him. Goethe hoped, without being entirely sure, that it would help Plessing recover his stability.

AUGUST

Shooting stars: Where are they racing? No sooner is the question asked, they're gone because we see in them the speed of arrows flying towards a mark.

The cricket chirp of the star-filled sky.

Around four in the morning, insistently, like cold water or a cold hand on my face—*Erlkönig*—after a very mild night.

§.

The pink of the lythrum: dark, related to reeds, to tall grasses, to marshes. Too dark to compare to flames.

Purple? They are 'only' flowers. I've been searching for the name for a long time.

At night's end: the powerful push of Orion's shoulder against the cold horizon, the press of winter's shoulder clearing a path over the mountain—as on other occasions you see large masses of white clouds rising slowly—like towers. The three giants of the underworld.

This slow, relentless march—yet it is only that of an unreal figure and a few crystalline landmarks.

SEPTEMBER

In this foggy nest of light

what is being hatched,

which egg?

DECEMBER

The other day, on the way to T., the violet forests on the slopes, a dark shade of violet, dense, reminiscent of the colour of certain mushrooms. And the low, thick clouds, the gaps in them moving over these same slopes.

A cloud of sleet passes over the gardens and meadows, blown so quickly by the north wind that you'd have thought you'd surprised a hunted phantom.

1983

Rereading Claudel's 'La Maison fermée' after many years. Although more than a little bloating here and there doesn't escape me and although the certainty of his declarations is foreign to me, I still admire the labouring energy of this slowly structured poetry—a little as if I were hearing the echo of a ceremony that was charged with meaning a long time ago, but in which I no longer think I could ever take part.

O. V. de L. Milosz. The small collection, *Poems*, that I bought in 1944 but hardly ever opened again. They are laments; they would be more touching if he didn't whine a bit too much and overdo the adjectives: 'poor, wounded birds', 'sad, grey coat', 'ancient cemeteries, serious and good'. The anthology, *The Berlin Carriage Stopped in the Night*, remains like a beautiful fragment of the narrative—and the three 'Symphonies', admirable almost end to end.

The stream flowing beneath a thin layer of ice: a mirror in which you'd see something other than your face.

Éluard in 1914:

> And whether the sky is miserable or transparent
> We cannot see it without loving it.

In these two mysteriously beautiful lines—despite or even because of their apparent banality—he had already found his tone to be best.

MARCH

One evening at Eautagnes: everything seemed suspended, the shadows of the trees on the grass seemed more weightless than ever, nothing could be understood, frail and poignant in its clarity. The village the colour of limestone.

In Doderer's *Demons*, the chapter 'At the Blue Unicorn' is one of the most beautiful and most convincing chapters in this curious book. It's one of those that make the most sense, that are most radiant: a radiance given off by the house itself, by the child, by Anna Kapsreiter, this woman of the people who says, when the child dies, 'Most important, is not to let yourself turn to stone.' The virtuosity of the passage about witches seems a bit superfluous compared to this. Here Doderer rejoins the Austria of Schubert and Stifter—if we can bring these two names together without being too arbitrary. Radiant intimacy, acceptance of reality—of which simple beings like Leonhard Kakabsa and Aloïs Gach are other examples. The author's predilection for these characters is, moreover, a very sensitive one.

Reread the *Letter of Lord Chandos*: this text from 1903 remains one of the most relevant on the crisis of the modern spirit. It elegantly expresses a profound drama: the loss of universal order or of all order, the need for a different, perhaps inaccessible, language to express this new experience—in which a watering can becomes more important than a lover, a moray eel more important than historical movements. What is odd is that Hofmannsthal's dramatic works respond so inadequately to this realization, as if he'd been unable to do more than find shelter under the roof of tradition and become a kind of official writer.

Thoughts? What thoughts?

Just the first call of the toad that blends with the night's warmth; a little later, the first scops owl.

At three in the afternoon, there was almost no visibility. The rain fell in sheets from grey clouds through which filtered only a sallow light. It's difficult to breathe under a roof that's too low. We must re-stitch almost continuously a fabric (life, ours) that's wearing thin, fraying. Without losing patience —we can't do much more than mend. Formal wear and finery are not for us, unless as a disguise.

There is a cold light peculiar to the rain, internal to it, oblique.

The last flowering trees in the garden—the tears.

The ruined church of Aleyrac. The small spiral carved into the stone that frames a niche in the apse is the only ornamentation aside from a violet at the base of the wall. The once-miraculous spring still flows, meagrely.

It's the time of season when in the still-bare forests the fresh, almost yellow, green of the beech trees appears, the folded leaf, hemmed with silver hairs, emerging from its light brown sheath.

A path of grass mixed with violets. It's also like a spring and no less miraculous.

MAY

Dream. This mountain in strong light feels like paradise. Hyenas approach, without inspiring the slightest fear; we play with them, throwing sticks as we could for dogs. We are, ourselves, no less astonished.

JUNE

I've always liked Persian miniatures; yet even more, in Aix the other evening, those two lively young sultanas, daughters of our friends, the K.s, who had come down for a few moments to charm us.

JULY

Dhôtel, in his *Rhétorique fabuleuse*:

> There is no world without another world that
> gives life to the most singular and necessary
> images.[12]

SEPTEMBER

From now on, listening only to the flowers' counsel,
antecedent to all knowledge . . .

NOVEMBER

> Voice foreign to the wood,
> or without echo, a bird
> that not more than once would
> in any lifetime be heard.

I don't read Mallarmé much any more, but these two
verses often return to me—like an indication of the
perceptions poetry sometimes allows. (A walk along
the Col de Valouse, bells of the goat herds among the
rocks, long grassy slopes of the Angèle mountain,
along which pass white clouds, come from the south
in very mild weather. Silence, immobility. Everything

seems to have been arranged with precision and deli-
cacy in this calmed space.)

1984

The path along the Col de l'Ancise descends between stones as white as marble that recall the seats in a Greek theatre under a light hardly subdued by the bare beech trees. It suddenly disappears in a kind of clearing on a rather steep slope where very old, dead chestnut trees still stand, the ground carpeted with parched heather. It creates a kind of scar or brand on the mountain slope, as if a giant hand of fire had rested there long ago with the ferocity of castigation. Crossing such sites bends the spirit towards the strange, the hidden, you seem to see more deeply or further, even the large farm lost in the bottom of the valley, the one you can truly say you stumble onto next, with dogs straining against their chains, stacks of firewood, the ground brown with wet sawdust, strong smells, machines covered with rust, and the dubious friendly remarks of the men who come out as we pass, seems strange, disquieting, truly wild. A partridge shoots out of the bushes that line the path, tall poplars tremble along the river; and the night's coolness grabs you like a state of intoxication while the sky turns metallic and winter's familiar stars multiply rapidly like sleet.

Astronomers recently discovered a very cold light scattered throughout the universe, a kind of 'fossilized' light that might be the residue of the infinitely more powerful light of origin. I note how close this is to what one is tempted to write about God, to feel when reading the Old Testament, for example. Our space, expanding, would become colder and more transparent while its initial compactness is opaque to our eyes.

In *Atoms of Silence*, Hubert Reeves writes that time passes more slowly at the bottom of a valley than on the top of a mountain.

At sunset, even as we feel the cold in the garden, an extremely thin, pointed moon appears above the horizon like a frigid blade, a fang, but that's badly expressed, because its wound, its sting in the heart, far from causing pain, brings delight. Later, it will appear more golden above a sky of deeper red.

Maybe a diamond, a glittering earring in the ear—pink with tenderness or desire—of a woman glimpsed during a celebration would have the same effect on the heart, a pang just as strong, that is, certainly painful. But I wouldn't be surprised if it were a sign, a hieroglyph taken from an even more distant language, thus the silent action, sudden, extremely brief, of a key made of crystal or ice; or the fall of a drop capable of assuaging one who is damned or dying.

As if someone suddenly spoke to you about a glacier suspended upon the nocturnal stone.

Schubert's Piano Sonata in B-flat Major (D. 960). In the first movement, that way of passing from one level to another in the space created by sounds, that progression, that other 'winter journey' towards whichever girl had been glimpsed but is never reached . . . Those pauses, those expectancies, those effusions. You could also see it as a drawing of hills in motion, beyond mountain ranges and passes—but also the house or room you'd dreamt of. Above all, there are those modulations that are like inflections of internal space, almost incomprehensibly exultant and poignant at the same time. This sends me back once again to the famous passage in Poe's 'Poetic Principle', quoted by Baudelaire, in which the author suggests that the particular emotion evoked by poetry, joy and sorrow combined, comes from the fact that it reminds us at once that something like Paradise exists and that we have been expelled from it. This merely defers the explanation.

Montagne Miélandre covered with snow, absolutely spotless: A monument to the memory of the swan? It's not a monument; it's a cloak (no matter that this has been said a hundred times), a coat of feathers, or it's a wing. It's as if one's gaze, in passing, despite the deterioration, finds shelter under a wing and so recovers childhood. Maybe that's what it is. Now that I look back from a distance, a distance of more than a year, finding again in memory that white clarity beneath a darker sky, I tell myself that it was something else again and very far: a blunting of the mountain's sharp edge, an attenuation of the earth, an ablution perhaps? The lamb the shepherd carries on his shoulders as our travelling companion carries his dog, its paws reddened by the ice, the one painted on the blue banners of the processions that, for a long time now, have no longer been possible or have been devoid of meaning?

FEBRUARY

Last night, again: the intense and frigid blue of the sky
above the snow that crowns the Montagne de la Lance
and lower down the very dark colours of the fields,
gardens, paths, as if concentrated. There is a connec-
tion there to water and to the moon, to the moon most
of all. Anything else? The snow, illuminated from
within, a mute, immobile clarity, and the depth of the
blues above and below. The swan. Again, the same
emotion, repeated without the slightest diminishment,
like a word of which one never tires because one will
never exhaust its meaning and because it seems to be
one of the most important words ever whispered in
your ear, or to your heart.

After five in the evening, when the sun nears the hori-
zon in a band of yellow sky, advancing sheets of rain
create an intense double rainbow against a blue back-
ground, one foot in the purple trees; then it disappears
like the slanting walls of rain.

André Dhôtel, *Rhétorique fabuleuse*. There are few
books articulating something like a philosophy, frag-
ments, elements of philosophy that speak to me more
persuasively, in other words, that are closer to what

I've been trying to think, to grasp through thought, starting from my own experiences. I retain a few essential statements.

First, Dhôtel presents a kind of *method* consisting of recognizing that we cannot know anything in advance, therefore we talk in order to know or, better, so that a breath will keep circulating and carry off all those who talk. Not even an expectation, much less an inquiry. A kind of pilgrimage, if we acknowledge as he does that the pilgrimage cannot have a goal, being rather 'a subtle science of wandering' because the goal is inaccessible.

On the other hand, far from pursuing harmony, a fabulous rhetoric would instead seek *divergence, dissonance, rupture* (of which Rimbaud gives the purest examples in his style as in his life) by means of which images appear and disappear. Because there is an unbridgeable distance between us and the outside light and it is this very distance that makes its power and radiance flare. Also, instead of believing in inspiration from within, one would have to always abandon oneself to this external power.

Along with this method, Dhôtel also expresses, after all, a kind of task, a duty: 'It is not a question of provoking the superstitious reveries with a kind of literature, only of perceiving around us certain traces of the dream that is completely real elsewhere, in order to prepare our gazes to welcome it one day.'

Of the pilgrim, he says: 'He must be taught to live in the space between knowledge and vision, and to take the precise steps that will lead him to the truth.'

Obviously, this non-knowledge of Dhôtel's seems to take on certain powerful certitudes that sustain his work, his life, even if they cannot be assimilated into his dogmas. Thus: 'There is no world without another world that gives life to the most singular and necessary images'; or again: 'Nothing is certain but presence and all presence worthy of the name is infinitely inexplicable . . . '; phrases that echo those of Paulhan in *Le Clair et l'obscur* (The Clear and the Obscure): ' . . . as if our world were next to some other world, usually invisible, but whose intervention in decisive periods alone could save ours from collapse.'[13]

The light emanating from this other world can only be glimpsed through rents, through intervals. It is like a flash that reaches us from 'a strange land' (yet not so strange that we cannot speak about it).

Let's admit it: no better 'explanation' of beauty has ever occurred to me; but it's hardly an explanation; it is, perhaps, simply one more metaphor for an insistent intuition, and likely to keep us from nihilism. Sometimes, however, the light no longer reaches our eyes. Or it seems to be a decoy, which absolutely does not fit Dhôtel's thought.

He insists on the necessity of speaking, that is of prolonging, of sustaining the conversation, which echoes Hölderlin: 'Man has learnt much since morning / since we have been a conversation and listen / to each other; but soon we will be song.' (Quote from 'Celebration of Peace' which Martin Buber interprets instead as: 'since we are something spoken—spoken by God'—which presupposes the utopia of a superior state of being, more harmonious, more ample); and Dhôtel adds: 'But the images of the beyond, even if we declare them dead (fairies or gods of Olympus), continue to feed the conversations because if these beings are not real, in our sense, who can assure us that they don't have respondents in a sky's ultimate clarity.' No inscription would be better suited to my *Landscape with Absent Figures*.

Another thought that gives me pause is the hypothesis of a world consisting of webs, hetero-geneous ones, perhaps, but which interact. Dhôtel offers as an example: 'For their departure, the swallows have tried to be contained by an unknown framework of space, let's say, by a complete dream that arose from an external order and not from themselves'; and the example of the rainbow: 'It's that the rain resembles a framework, but the rainbow, completely different from this framework, enters it to form a kind of fabric of another nature altogether. And the simple image of the rainbow becomes fabulous from the mere fact that it offers us a superimposed vision that is perfectly explicable but still renews all things. Because the world then no longer appears infrangible or finished, but filled with various and unsuspected weavings that are occasionally manifest.'

All this keeps me marvellous company until the point when suffering declares itself and devastates—and tears apart all these webs, at least for me—without, however, allowing another light to appear.

Iris one foot in the copse
slender and sometimes
enveloped in twists
of hail . . .

(Moon in broad daylight)

A scale of fine nacre
or phantom of a star in daytime
or flake in the process of melting . . .

Reading Dhôtel led me back to the *Illuminations*, which I haven't reread in years. I'm surprised at how many lines stayed in my memory, just buried under others, as if they were imprinted very deep within me; I find them as fresh, as distinctive as I did in adolescence, without having faded in the least; defying all the imitations I'd been subjected to since. A torrent's violent haste.

Henri Thomas in *Le migrateur* (The Migrant):

> All endeavours, all acts of selflessness do not have the same merit. There is only one good kind of endeavour, those that result in something that I alone am capable of creating and that is also valuable for others. They teach me that I am not alone, good news. It is because each person can create something unique that communion occurs . . .

Later:

> It's a matter of choosing what's most complex, most improbable, least reducible to a formula . . .

Or again:

> . . . I have no liking to express anything but the stubborn kernel of obscurity that is my very being, my moral and poetic substance . . . And yet, how can one express (*how to* say!) the recognition, the hope, the joy that fills me when true communication occurs,

most often through a book, in passages where that extraordinarily peaceful remote land appears to me and which I am the only one to visualize . . .

With regard to 'great readings':

'It's true' and even 'It's beautiful' always mean: there is something to do here, 'in real life'.

Finally, along the same lines, something I've often said, scarcely differently:

This love of poetry was naturally passed on through books, but in the way the gaze passes through a skylight to discover the sky, the sea, living bodies . . . [14]

Dull, grey weather, like bad prose, as if the world had no more 'soul', as if the sky were the wall lining a street down which the wind blows violently, but with a mechanical, empty violence.

Morandi. I don't think any other painter worked with poorer, more humble material; not even Chardin, not even Cézanne. It's a kind of miracle to have created such beautiful works from two or three objects that are for the most part undistinguished, not even elegant, and with such a restrained palette. What we know of the painter's life illuminates this mystery somewhat. He hardly read, it is said, but he often reread: Pascal and Leopardi. He lived a monkish life. What did he want to say or what was expressed through him over the course of those silent, patient years, devoted solely to his work? How did he manage to avoid drying up in the monotonous company of these objects, how did he keep from wanting to throw them out the window at least once? Would it be overly literary to suppose that he grouped them together like timid creatures so they could better resist destruction? And those delicate colours, those pinks, mauves, ochres, ivories, how did they not turn insipid or cloying? I wonder how one can speak of the canvases from the end of his life, his most beautiful to my mind. I will leave my opinion of his landscapes to the side to address what is most singular, perhaps essential; because the sway a landscape, a nude, a portrait can have over us is not so strange; nor is that of most still lifes, for that matter, just like Chardin's because of the fruits, the flower, the violins in them. But when one is faced with this extreme of poverty, here, in his paintings done after 1943, still more in those painted after the war—and the word 'poor' is not fitting, because it could evoke a social state, difficult or pitiful fates, and therefore pathos, whereas it is rather a question of apparent insignificance—? What can be said about them?

First: that they discourage any commentary.

The things these still lifes show—though hardly —are immobile, temperate, restrained without being rigid. Trapped, perhaps, but living. They recall poet monks in Japan through their humble poverty, the white bowl or what could be an inkwell. These things are not polished nor shiny; one senses the discreet grain of the canvas. Nor are they surrounded: their contours tremble, hesitate. There are shadows. There are passages, muted modulations. Modest objects are moved together, gathered, but not jumbled. We don't see them here in their daily roles. They have been 'composed', prepared patiently, even, as if out of a desire that they soothe the gaze, the heart. But perhaps there wasn't even this desire. It's like a magical procedure performed by silence without any paraphernalia, beyond any state of trance; a 'domestication' in the etymological sense.

Everything seems to be lit by a familiar lamp. Even if the colours are often those of dawn, they don't evoke daybreak; they don't evoke 'anything else'. (Nor any lyricism.) Colours that seem enamoured with themselves, in happy harmony. Despite this poverty or this economy of effects and subjects, despite what I've been told about the painter, I don't want to use the word asceticism. It's simply tender and familiar, yet it remains all the while infinitely mysterious and distant. There is an almost maternal magic or the grace preserved by an elderly servant of the house: 'the kind-hearted servant of whom you were jealous' . . .

Morandi needs nothing: no events, mythological or otherwise, no vast landscapes, or human presences —much less symbols; and his painting is no less human for it. He calms as a blessing once did, not as a sedative. He assembles the way we meditate. The word 'meditation' is indicated here more than in any other painting. He speaks with tenderness, occasionally with a certain severity, but without coldness. In this context, the word 'paternal' also comes to mind. It's curious that on the subject of this solitary man, I've used the two words 'paternal' and 'maternal'.

To understand this art, one must imagine the painter endowed with an attention and perseverance that greatly exceed ordinary abilities.

MARCH

I saw the mountain again like a cape with snowy shoulders, which I would gladly don today, as if I were entering into its order. An order of the greatest serenity. This heavy, opaque, massive, hard thing now appears weightless, to be no heavier than the feather of snowy owl. It looks as if it could no longer wound or crush, as if it were nothing more than slightly thickened sky. Once again, the image of what we dream, like the ostention (this word doesn't exist—well, too bad) of a Host. May death be no more dense than it is or than its appearance today. I read this today in the wide-open book of the sky; I listened to the teaching of the epistle. It was just a state of water become visible in the air, in the blue, water grown soft, woolly, calm; like silence, also. It was rather something between the words inscribed in the book of the sky, silence made tangible through extreme softness. A lamb? (I will come back to this . . .) Maybe it truly resembled the lamb on the blue banners of processions long ago? The almost imperceptible bleating of the snow.

'The Structure of Myths' by Mircea Eliade: 'The man of the societies in which myth is a living thing lives in a World that, though "in cipher" and mysterious is "open". The World "speaks" to man . . . '[15] He becomes transparent.

This is most certainly exactly what the poetic experience restores to us; we would then simply be backward, not to say imbecile, children.

Easter. Beautiful warm days, without wind.

Late at night, as I was descending the stairs, I saw our neighbour's small window illuminated and, just above her roof, a yellow-ochre moon and two large stars (or planets) like straw.

Youthful grace, clarity. It's like opening the pages of the *Vita Nuova* again: 'A ciascun alma presa e gentil core'; or rereading the sonnet to Guido Calvacanti in *Rime*: 'Guido, I with that you and Lapo and I', knowing that one can never board this boat again, except as a shade mingling invisibly with the laughter, the songs, the pleasures that it rocks on the sparkling water. Petrarch is not far either. One believes one is nearing the fairy's reign. Each holds a leafy branch, which transforms you when they brush you with it. In their gaze is a water that is believed to heal or transmit a refreshing inebriation.

The cherry trees are now little more than plumes of snow. The bees, themselves rapid and numerous, won't be long in communicating this. There is a golden humming in the air like that of an immense swarm.

Monteverdi's vocal music is also in harmony with these bracing or burning constellations.

Through the fig tree, still barely adorned with leaves, like a pink-grey filter: the afternoon light. Yet is it really a filter, a grill, a web? I would say, rather, that the tree itself resembles lignified, nascent, brittle, 'acerbic' light. Or else it reminds me of a candelabra whose leaves would be lit. Behind it, I see not just the April light but another that one could believe came from a space farther away.

> Guido, I wish that you and Lapo and I
> could be conveyed by some enchantment
> into a vessel blown by every wind . . .

For a moment, I dreamt we were in this vessel,
I even heard laughter, heard songs
that swarm in the trees in April . . .
but look at your hands! And bid them instead
to board the other vessel with you instead, the black
    one,
if they consent and turn the fog away

or better: consent to be no more than an attentive
    shadow
between their songs, like the remains of winter
in the Easter air.

Dhôtel: 'It's like a beam of light that comes to us from a foreign land.'

The cherry trees illuminate more for me than thought. They are the scribes of my Orphic lamella. There is a trace in the earth, dug deep by a musician's finger.

The spirit of the madrigal, a word I associate in dreams with *madrugada*, dawn in Spanish, the moment when night is ending and the point the crest of night becomes inflamed, the hour of the colour pink beneath the sky's skin.

There are three women in one garden
for whom the sun's last light
smokes like incense
to the point where we see almost nothing more than
    their dresses in this glory

And the first iris to the new iris
as if it had been offered
a bell cast from the blue of the sky

as if I offered it
some sky to breathe

Crowns of linaria. All around there are crowns light
enough for their brow.

JUNE

Fragment of a dream, the only one that remains: we're
five men, rather wretchedly dressed, probably gath-
ered together to be sent to a camp or prison (every-
thing is hazy in my memory, but maybe it was so in
the dream as well). One of them is Yves Bonnefoy:
because he dropped his identification papers, I pick
them up and read his name—*Barstein*; and so I say, or
say to myself: no surprise that that's his name because
in German it means 'bare stone' (thinking of his vol-
ume, *Written Stone*). And I add, speaking to someone,
that I'm proud to be there with these four Jews. It's
extremely odd that I remembered, in the dream, if it
was in fact so, the meaning of the word *bar*, whereas I
had to check it in the dictionary when I woke.

§

At midday, suddenly, two swifts very high in the sky next to a cloud shaped like a white, weightless tower—like some kind of devastating, enigmatic apparition or a measure of the air's elevation, a revelation of aerial space, an iron arrow in the heart. A strange joy of less than a second—and in rereading what I've written, I remember the gyrfalcon of *The Solitudes*, 'bizarre scandal of the air'—a letter written on the blue, then erased, a line—or the barb of a fishhook? Does anyone know who could have showed you this way?

§

Dream. My mother has left the house one night midwinter and I am alone. I struggle to cross a curtain of snow-covered trees. She must be in a church or in a car; the possibility of an accident occurs to me. I go to a neighbouring farm for help where they are hesitant to assist. I no longer have the slightest doubt that my mother is dead.

Over the course of the same night, in another dream, I walked for a long time in an unrecognizable Lausanne which had become a city of stunning beauty, not unrelated to the cities in the *Illuminations*: water flows rapidly down a narrow, steeply inclined stone channel, there are terraces, vaulted passages, cleresto-ries, empty hollow blocks of flats of which only the ancient facades have been preserved, tierings, and one side with a 'suspended garden' as the real city might have, but magnified, transfigured in an eternal light.

JULY

This summer is very golden, very beautiful; wheat that is more orange than blond has been stacked in the combes as in the bottom of a goblet, like heat in the palm of a hand. The wild oats seem lighter and paler than ever; weighing little but still bound to the burning ground; dry but not arid; pale but not bloodless.

Monteverdi's *Lettera amorosa*: 'Altro già non son io che di vostra beltà preda e trofeo', and those 'snow-covered paths' at the end of the madrigal that I always hear, not as the precious metaphor for white skin that they, in fact, are (although this image remains vaguely in the background to enrich the emotions even more), but as the actual thing they name and that is, beyond all metaphor, the term most charged with meaning and dreams.

The gleam, the labyrinth, the forest of hair.

Claudio Monteverdi. He is perhaps one of the only musicians whose melodies burn (with 'languor': *languidi miei sguardi*). It's like fire in the garden, which the wind torments, obscures and fans in turn. If I think of an air by Bach, I picture it rising freely and directly, then expanding at high altitude; with Monteverdi, the air seems to me to be held out towards someone elusive or at least not yet apprehended—someone like a shadow walking through a forest? And who must be called, called back at any price, before it's too late. The intensity of the call sets the voice alight and it is in the light from its conflagration that the world—if there still is a world—appears.

(In Schubert's *Lieder* there can also be an impulse towards another; but it is, one would say, an impulse of the heart rather than the body, more enveloped in shadows and melancholy, a gentle light rather than fire.)

The sour cherry tree is covered with fruit: a Persian miniature, our friend J. E. notes with his customary aptness. A very particular shine, like enamel. The fruit are of rutilant colour, but are also like nearly translucent marbles. Numerous, light. An encounter impossible to translate into another. As soon as blood or rubies come up, we are led astray. And so? What must be added to the word cherry? to the word red? to the word fruit? A sultana to pick them?

Claudio in old age, for whom does he still fashion the inflamed whorls of his melodies? Is he completely prey to an illusion or is there something behind that illusion?

Mörike: *Mozart's Journey to Prague*, a novella of transparent grace, worthy of its subject. His picking an orange, out of sheer absentmindedness, in a nobleman's park, not only affords Mozart and his wife a pleasant stay in the castle but also reminds him of a nautical spectacle he saw in Naples as a child, a kind of pantomime in which oranges were gracefully tossed from one boat to another, one carrying five attractive young women and five young men in red, the other carrying the same dressed in green, playing this game in honour of Eros; as for me, reading this, I thought of the invocation of the two 'musical' boats in Góngora's *Second Solitude*, as I was, at the time, revising my translation of it. And it seemed to me that an unexpected link bound the two, and with Dante's cheerful poem to Guido Calvacanti, all these boats, all these celebrations, bathed in the same summer light as I was, in the transfiguration of poetry.

The constellation of the Boat
placed in the same rank as the others one night only
in the mountains
raised to the same height as the others
projected from the heart

Once again, in the middle of summer, I see tendrils of bindweed climbing up, beginning to climb up, like bonds or chains, the rosebush now without flowers. And I say to myself: Thus does age rise in us and not just autumn in summer. And I wish it would blossom one last time in a few pink fires.

He who writes will be like someone who fills a goblet with all the light of summer, with all that was in summer, then lifts it up so it will shine in his hand—with all it contains—which he will have to express before the frost reaches his fingers.

For the day's fan is already folding up.

A little before six in the morning, the nightjar's rattle moves off quite far. It snaps its wings loosely: a slap of wet laundry. The gloom, the black trees. It's only when the sky turns pink that the winged flutes set in. Before there was that wooden instrument or those rapid little wooden hammers—and the Pleiades still vaguely visible.

Clouds: large feathery letters or suspended beds.

Essentially, the mountains are made from several blue waters.

Then things imperceptibly become visible, precise, almost disappointing in the moment.

AUGUST

At the end of the August night, one notices the winter constellations again with surprise: the Charioteer with Capella like a tall house, the Pleiades above the silvered crowns of the trees and the Montagne de la Lance. Next, I recognize Orion like a warrior slowly rising from his grave. Rarely have I seen a more pellucid end of night. And when the light hits the vegetation, the blue hills in the distance are, with the greenery, of Poussin at his most mythological.

At the break of day, a breath weakly lifts the foliage.

Warbler
last speaking bird in midsummer
what is you are telling me now and then
in the leaves of the linden?
What can a voice so limpid be saying?

Only a glance can resemble this water

Wearing a halo of gentle bees without stingers
or with the clarity of a forest dawn

Saint Sebastian, bound by invisible chains
to an absent column,
but become the archer
who wounds with arrows that are also invisible.

SEPTEMBER

The chapel in Plaisians, in the Baronnies, encircled with beehives like tombs: and if we imagined the reverse?

1985

Having finally obtained a favourable answer from a young woman I had long loved in vain in the past, I suddenly hear my father in the corridor repeating several times in a stammering voice I don't recognize as his, the words 'to the office'; no less suddenly, I find I'm alone again in the room with yellow wallpaper I had as an adolescent in L. A wave of anxiety had barely begun to wash over me before I stumble over him, lying on his back across my doorstep, his mouth full of blood. I take in this horrible situation, but also notice that he's not dead and I ask that a doctor be called as quickly as possible as my mother comes running.

Awake, I'm surprised at having passed so quickly from the extreme sweetness of an old love to this menace. In the garden, where a few patches of snow remain, the vague reddening of the sky blends with this sweetness returned in dream.

'Once again the moon speaks to the snow . . . ' But one always wishes these beams of light would take shape, these words become palpable.

Sting, diamond: my signs this past winter and, behind me, snow on the summit in the mountains' tender, mysterious blue. Weapons, jewels, pins for the shadow seen fleeing at night's end, the shadow that cannot be held back, that will not turn on you. Crescent moon or finery for bare skin, denuded by night, but that is also a kind of call, nearly mute, a sigh escaped from a too distant mouth.

Sometimes you believe you're walking in another, an unknown space that nevertheless is your native land.

MARCH

Linden flowering with limpid water.

APRIL

Purcell's 'Music for a While' sung by Alfred Deller.

'Music, an instant . . .' in summer's nocturnal centre, in a place you might remember, one night you might be able to date, an instant . . . But was it one more thing we can name so easily, an instant we can call a moment? Is not all consummate music another kind of time insinuated into enumerable time or a transformation of it into a higher, more perfect measure, and therefore the indication of possible completion, hence our emotion when we hear it?

> The voice was like a bird come from
>   elsewhere,
> rising and falling, twirling in the native air.
> The voice was tenderness, fear, solitude,
> and quenched your thirst without depriving
>   you of it . . .

> There was that late winter, saturated with frigid lights as if we were already being pursued by a swarm of hail with most tender stings.
>
> Then the knot of brooks came undone like a braid.
>
> The hail lived in the trees for a short time . . .

Night. Nightingales or amorous brooks.

The warm beauty of a bereaved summer's end.

My father died on the third, almost out of care-lessness, a carelessness fostered by extreme weariness. The 7 September, in the middle of those fields still as marvellous as when he crossed them long ago on horseback, then by motorcycle, there was a kind of icy cloak around the chapel in Curtilles in which the sounds of the oboes and the large flowers picked from a country garden seemed to mingle like vines around a void similar to a mournful column.

When we dry up, do we reach the very bones of the mystery that we are? It may be that we come to love skin more and more.

Music, glances, the touch of hands. The milky light in which the world is bathed right now, as if everything had become a herd resting in vast prairies, as if everything were saturated with dew and mist, enveloped in wool.

Death and the Maiden.

Face still intact in the fleecy light, equally distant, but so clear that an afternoon moon was visible.

Hide a moment longer this hirsute death, this finished thing, like all of us to some degree, poorly loving, poorly loved.

OCTOBER

Suddenly glimpsed from the depths of the Rochecour-bière grotto between the trunks of enormous water oaks, the moon's light, not the celestial body itself, resembles fog; and when you get up in surprise and move closer to it, the entire poplar grove appears, coated in silver, still hardly real.

We were there because some young Germans our friends knew were trying to work themselves into a trance under the grotto's rocky awning by inter-minably beating African drums. They turned their backs to the valley. Is it worth pursuing uncertain visions, sometimes paying with one's life, if it means not seeing marvels that are within reach, missing encounters with real fairies?

NOVEMBER

A poem by Emily Brontë, read in a translation by Pierre Leyris, one of our best and most generous ferrymen across the English Channel.

Fall, leaves, fall; die, flowers, away;
Lengthen night and shorten day;
Every leaf speaks bliss to me
Fluttering from the autumn tree.

I shall smile when wreaths of snow
Blossom where the rose should grow;
I shall sing when night's decay
Ushers in a drearier day.[16]

DECEMBER

The comet, sparkling, observed yesterday in the icy
night: nothing more than a dandelion's feathery
sphere.

1986

JUNE

The word 'linden', well suited to the buzzing of the bees over their flowers and to the image of a dry rain made of pollen and dust. Whoever picks it is prisoner of a perfumed constellation; thus does one sometimes dream of burrowing into a crackling head of hair.

A tree like a blond shelter, like a swarm of disarmed bees; for several days of ease, disarmed.

Those moments in life when the sting is what is most tender and most desired. 'A land of milk and honey': such is the lover, languorous, brushed over in a dream or with one's hands.

I listen again to the 'Linden Tree' in 'Winterreise'. *Lindenbaum*: the German word is more caressing than *tilleul*; *linde* can also mean 'soft'. This world like a balm for the ear. And, in the song, the tree is the voyager's stopping point, his longed-for haven, the rest also described in Goethe's famous poem 'Wayfarer's Night Song', but is, in the end, the peace of death.

Borges writes in 'The Wall and the Books' (in *Labyrinths*):

> Music, states of happiness, mythology, faces belabored by time, certain twilights and certain places try to tell us something, or have said something we should not have missed, or are about to say something; this imminence of a revelation which does not occur is, perhaps, the aesthetic phenomenon.[17]

Also from Borges, these beautiful lines on rain:

> Quite suddenly the evening clears at last
> as now outside the soft small rain is falling.
> Falling or fallen. Rain itself is something
> undoubtedly which happens in the past.[18]

OCTOBER

A poem by Emily Dickinson:

> Where every bird is bold to go,
> And bees abashless play,
> The foreigner before he knocks
> Must thrust the tears away.[19]

['Où chaque oiseau a licence d'aller
Et les abeilles jouent sans honte,
L'étranger avant de frapper
Doit essuyer ses larmes.']*

The poem holds your attention before you've understood it, before you've even tried to understand it, perhaps because of the proximity of playing and tears, of the open space and the closed door. You feel a similar sense of wonder at certain haikus in which the most humble objects serve as keys opening onto profound spaces. Then, when you ask what these verses are about, you hesitate.

I imagine that Emily Dickinson, herself close to birds and bees through her lightness and vivacity, discreetly invites us—if we want to find the 'entryway into the garden' (of Jourdan), 'the key to the ancient banquet' (of Rimbaud)—to be free of ourselves, to wash away our sorrows, always too turbid for the open air.

---

* Having read this (complete layman's) note in a journal, Claire Malroux helpfully informs me that 'thrust' is much stronger than *essuyer* [wipe], and here means 'to chase away', if not 'force back'; and that the 'foreigner' is more than an *étranger* [stranger] (almost an intruder)? [This is Jaccottet's translation.—Trans.]

The constellation of the Boat
raised to the height of the others for one
    summer night
in the mountains

I thought I saw it glide,
laden with graceful shades,
through the sparse, frigid grasses . . .

Much later I saw
the old smith of whorls and flames
set down his tools:
all his courtly glory,
his patient science
rendered futile in an instant
against this ember that leapt up against his
    heart.

Was he delirious when I heard him murmur:
'If this lamp so like a beehive is taken away
    from me,
if this fragrance fades, my friends,
you can take away these white ties and these
    feathers:
where I am awaited, I will have no more
    need of them . . . '

Much rereading over the past two years, of Goethe, late Goethe, inspired mostly by Pietro Citati's book. A collection of more recent writings by my compatriot, the novelist Adolf Muschg, *Goethe als Emigrant*, shows I'm not alone in my renewed interest. This fifty-four-year-old writer presents Goethe—for so long dismissed in favour of Hölderlin, Kleist or Rilke—as a Green *avant la letter*, a man who accepts the world as it is, a man attached to the world in its totality, a man of openness as well; which brings him close to the younger Peter Handke discussing Cézanne, the Handke of the 'slow homecoming'. In his own reflections on Goethe, Muschg sees an element of a last attempt, one that is perhaps already too late, to save a world threatened with annihilation.

With regard to the *West-Eastern Divan*. When Goethe undertook this venture, he was sixty-five years old. In this new poetic endeavour, he was trying to rejuvenate himself by drinking from a still-refreshing stream, to broaden himself in time and space. Once more, he showed himself to be open and audacious.

Once more, as rife with references as he was, he nourished his lyricism with his life circumstances: numerous poems are dated like entries in an intimate journal. Thus, many of those that make up the first book of the compilation, 'The Book of the Singer', were written on the journey that took Goethe in July and August 1814 from Weimar to Frankfurt, the town of his birth, which he hadn't see for twenty years. On the 26 August, for example, he writes nine poems that he later distributes throughout various books of the *Divan*.

It seems to me that no translation will ever be able to convey the serene perfection Goethe attains in this work. How can one translate these two brief lines, as sober and luminous as an inscription?

> Schöpft des Dichters reine Hand,
> Wasser wird sich ballen?

They are the echo of an Indian legend that evokes a woman so pure of heart that she can carry water home in the palms of her hands without needing any vessel, yet she loses this power as soon as she feels temptation at the sight of an angel's reflection in the water:

> In the poet's pure hand
> does water curl into a ball?
> > Form a sphere?
> > Condense to a globe?

As an example of Goethe combining life circumstances with cultural references, this poem of 1815 to

greet Marianne von Willemer when he arrived in
Frankfurt:

> How blessed was I!
> I wandered through the land
> Where the hoopoe crosses my path.
> I sought shells of ancient seas
> Petrified in rock;
> The hoopoe came running
> Spreading his crest
> Preening with a teasing air,
> Full of life,
> He mocked the dead.
> 'Hudhud,' I said, 'you are,
> Indeed, a beautiful bird.
> Make haste, my hoopoe!
> Hurry to my beloved
> And tell her I
> Am hers for ever.
> You also played the part
> So long ago
> Of go-between
> For Salomon and Sheba's queen!'

(And here we note that the dead things mocked by the
hoopoe are the fossils the wanderer is searching for.)
Four years later, Marianne von Willemer will write:
'On a walk with Boisserée, our path led us through a

forest bathed in a marvellous light by the setting sun in which holly grew thickly; its golden greenery illuminated by the sun against a background of shadow evoked the luxuriousness of the south; and, in fact, a hoopoe crossed the path, then perched, immobile, on a holly bush. I drew near it and said . . . no, I didn't say anything to it, it already knows everything.' Marianne ordered a walking stick decorated with the carved figure of a hoopoe as a gift for Goethe in 1819. This object can still be seen in his study on the Frauenplan.

(*Later.*) Everything I observed in 1986 and have just reread two years later, definitely defies translation*— at least my powers of translation—especially since it's more beautiful, like the poem 'Summer Night' in the 'Book of the Cupbearer':

> Wenn sie sich einander loben,
> Jene Feuer in dem Blauen.
>
> [When they praise each other,
> those fires in the blue.]

---

* When the 'Marienbad Elegy' and a few other, rarely found poems were published in 1993 in the collection *Poetry / Gallimard*, translated by Jean Tardieu, I was all the happier to have these claims disproven by a translator who is a friend and whose work is important to me.

The walks, the ideas, the echoes of very old poems, the woes and the joys of love (the prison of curls, once again, after Monteverdi's *Lettera amorosa* and before *La Chevelure*, so ardently celebrated by Baudelaire), the summer night, space, all that appears to Goethe resting in God's hand, all this in the most beautiful of these poems is the object of a supreme decantation. All is good because all is in God. And because all is good, words are no more than a light, sovereign game, an elfin dance in the most serene light that ever was.

In his commentary on the *Divan*, Ernst Beutler quotes from Hermann Grimm's account of his visits to the elderly Marianne von Willemer, in which he laments the loss of the point of conversation and concludes: 'We live with our eyes glued to our watch.' Around 1855! What a strange sentiment it is: that the past was better, life healthier, virtue more respected, and so on. Are there any chroniclers, writers of memoirs, historians, or moralists who, grown old, don't consider the world worse than when they were young or, as they say, 'back in the day'?

A quote from Henry Corbin, discovered on the cover of a poetry magazine: 'Perhaps the only trace left after an apparition of the invisible is a sonorous incantation perceptible only to the heart's ear.'

1987

Schelling wrote *Clara* between 1810 and 1813. (In 1810, Hölderlin is in his tower, in the carpenter Zimmer's house—forty years earlier, Schelling had been one of his few childhood friends.) Schelling wrote this slender work, left unfinished, with a tone that recalls Plato's dialogues, after the death of his wife, Caroline.

Four speakers: a pastor, a doctor, a monk, and Clara, who has just lost her husband. The book begins in an autumn light of All Souls' Day: 'Deserts, mountains, distant lands, and seas can separate us from a friend in this life; the distance between this life and the other is no greater than that between night and day or vice versa. A heartfelt thought, together with our complete withdrawal from anything external, transfers us into that other world, and perhaps this other world becomes all the more hidden from us, the nearer to us it is . . .'[20]

The pastor, however, evinces a prudent reserve towards this dream of an easy passage between the two realms: 'I let justice be done to the warmth of each beautiful heart, only let us take care not to shape the inspiration of feelings and the inventions of longing into general truths; for then there will no longer be any divisions . . . '

Thus they converse gravely in the autumn light. Schelling is not writing a treatise on death; he weaves a web of reflections around Clara's bereavement in an attempt to reconcile her, little by little, with the world by considering the link, the passage between nature and spirit, like that between the living and the dead.

The doctor explains that man is 'the turning point' between the world of nature and the spirit world and interprets the myth of Orpheus in his own way: nature's elevation 'rested on whether he would forget what was behind him and reach towards what lay before him'. Instead of becoming attached only to the external world, man should have freed himself from it in order to move towards its progressive internalization (a process in which I find a distant echo of the ninth 'Duino Elegy': 'Earth, isn't this what you want: an invisible re-arising is us? Is it not your dream / to be one day invisible? Earth! invisible!'[21]) His failure to fulfil this office brought on a catastrophe: 'the whole Earth is one great ruin,' man is bewitched. 'Because of this, heaven sent higher beings from time to time, who were supposed to undo the spell within his inner being and to open up to him a glance into the higher world again with their wonderful hymns and magic charms.'

Christmas, when the bond between the higher and the lower is traditionally renewed, provides a pretext for a dialogue about higher states of consciousness: 'when you are in such a state it seems as if your whole being were unified in One focal point, as if it were one light, one flame'. These states are transitory: What is one to do in the interval? Engage in activity, piece together the surviving fragments, retain it as a memory 'through clear concepts'.

Further on, after death has been defined as the elevation of man 'into a higher potency' (in the mathematical sense), come Clara's remarks; 'And I don't know, she continued, but the day's splendour and magnificence seem so external to me, and only when they disappear does what is truly internal emerge; but why does it have to be night?—The night shows, I answered, that what is truly internal within us is still unfulfilled and that for us this belongs to the future and to what is hidden.—If a light were to dawn within night itself, she continued, so that a nightlike day and a daylike night embraced us all, then all our wishes would find their final resting place. Is that why, she added, a moonlit night touches our inner being in such a wonderfully sweet way . . . ?' We believe we can hear Novalis, of course, but also the Musil of the beginning of the second part of *The Man without Qualities*; and later, when Schelling opposes 'those having their last sleep' to 'those who have fallen asleep', those in their final sleep are the happy ones who have escaped earthly slumber, and again we think of Rilke in the *Duino Elegies*, of 'those who died young.'

In another section, Schelling condemns the philosophers' jargon and defends the simple, mundane language that characterizes his own endeavour: 'The deepest, I feel, must also be the clearest; just as what is clearest, e.g., a crystal, by virtue of being such, doesn't seem to get closer to me, but instead seems to withdraw and to become more obscure, and just as I can look into a drop of water as if into an abyss. At any rate, depth must be distinguished from opacity . . . '

The fourth section of the book, 'at a time bordering between winter and spring', unites even more directly thought processes with a place that meditators contemplate with emotion, a lake, 'a picture of the past, of eternal peace, and isolation.' About places, the doctor notably says: 'Even a locality hides its own secret [. . .] Weren't even the ancients' oracles tied to certain areas, even to particular places, and shouldn't we draw the general conclusion from this that locality isn't as irrelevant to the higher as is generally supposed? Indeed, don't we feel a certain spiritual presence in every place, which either attracts us to that place or puts us off? The same also applies to individual periods of time.'

Finally, a few lines later: 'But why does it happen so seldom, Clara said, and why does it seem to be so difficult for a person's inner being to be opened up to him through which he can, indeed, constantly be in a relationship to a higher world?—It is, I said, like other gifts that are shared out according to favour and not to merit and through which God often raises what's lower and held in low esteem. But there is one secret in particular that most people won't grasp: that those who want such a gift will never share in it, and that the first condition for it is composure and a quiet will.'

There is no doubt that if this book took such hold of me, it is inextricably because of both its central theme—the link and the passage between the two realms—and its tone. As if this tone were necessary to treat the subject properly.

Discourses of Rumi, a collection of the great thirteenth-century mystic's conversations with his disciples.

All things in his world are masks and veils: 'If God's beauty were to appear unveiled, we could not endure it . . . '

He returns to the theme of the moth and the flame in his particular way: 'If the moth throws itself into the candle's flame and is not consumed, then it is no candle.' 'It is God who consumes human beings, annihilating them, and reason cannot grasp Him.' I thought again of one of the best-known poems in the *Divan*. Goethe's 'Blessed Longing', which was inspired by Saadi:

> Tell it only to the wise
> For the crowds will mock,
> I wish to praise what is alive
> Yet longs to die in the flame . . .

Rumi again: 'A person is seated, awake through a dark night, intending to leave at daybreak. Even though he does not know how he will travel, in waiting for day, he approaches day. Thus, someone who follows a caravan through the dark, foggy night, advances without knowing where he will arrive, what places he will pass, or what distance he will cover. But when day comes, he will see where his journey has led him and will have arrived somewhere.'

Man: 'If he does not speak outwardly, he speaks inwardly. He is constantly speaking, like a torrent clouded with mud. The clear water is his speech and the clay is his animality, but the clay in him is accidental.'

Did I not live, that year? Or did I live too much to have a head clear enough to write anything? Sometimes, indeed, we pass through the world like a phantom: it's an offence against the world, against those who are with you, and against everything invisible.

1988

Sono soltanto quelle anime in pena . . .

(*There are only those souls in pain, those bees,
ranging from tree bark to tree bark in this desert
that is winter . . .*)

It's the voice of Mario Luzi in 'The Bees', a poem in
the collection *From the Depths of Countryside* which
also includes four admirable poems in memory of his
mother. *Christian Death* is one of these: 'la voce di
colei che come serva fedele' seems a reminiscence of
Dante.

MARCH

Jouve's handwriting (he has inscribed several things
for me); that fine, tiny writing, extraordinarily con-
trolled, those straight lines, those perfectly equal

spaces have something strange about them, even disturbing in their lack of spontaneity and breadth. Perhaps that explains in part the failure of his verse.

I like the theatre, but I don't care for poems or narratives that erect a theatre on the page as is often the case when an erotic obsession guides the writer (as with Jouve, as a matter of fact, or with Mandiargues, for example). The same applies to rambles out of doors:

> Bricks and tiles
> Oh charming covers
> Intimate retreats
> For the lovers!

which are no wiser, but which allow you to breathe. (I think it was the 'confining' aspect of many of Balthus' paintings that I found unpleasant in the Beaubourg retrospective. Even his mountains are airless: they're the cramped setting of an obsession. A family flaw!)

I would like to write a salute to Schehadé, who never cast a shadow on these pages; like those late poems by Borges in *The Conjured Ones* of so crystalline a melancholy, they almost give you wings:

We live discovering and forgetting
That sweet habit of night.
Look at it carefully. It might be your last.

(It must be said that Claude Estaban has served this writing as well as Ibarra did it a disservice, which Jacques Réda had also noted when that unfortunate volume appeared.)

Zurbarán: monumental and silent, imposing silence (before anything else). Calm grandeur, solidity, true majesty, without grandiosity or excess. *Saint Serapion* is a monument to restrained suffering.

After this, one can't deny a kind of majesty—sculptural and strange—to the *Demoiselles d'Avignon* as well.

APRIL

Hölderlin fragments: it's mistaken and pretentious to use these texts—obscure because incomplete, unfinished—as justification for writing incomplete, obscure texts oneself.

One of the many lessons in style that Baudelaire can offer is the particularly magical combinations of several words:

> It is She! dark and yet luminous . . .
> . . . .
> Many jewels lie buried . . .
> . . . .
> In kisses of satin and linen . . .

Crest trails, spiked with stony ridges, trails for goats, on which one is easily reduced to cowering. Between winter and summer, in the last cold spells, the last fogs. There's something to be said about these dangers as long as things remain enveloped in fog, in cold sweat, amid trees that are still bare but ready to open their green fans, to offer shelter . . .

A short time later, several days later, everything is cloaked, protected, feathered; weighed down. Will memory be able to retain what preceded, the forest's rigging without sails just before the troop's thousand wings unfurl to take flight; just before the eyelid rises?

J. F. Billeter, in an article from 1986, 'Chinese Poetry and Reality', articulates propositions which fit my experience exactly: that we seek shelter from the real behind schema (which are, for that matter, in many respects useful, necessary, even fruitful) and that to rejoin the real, we need to break with our mental habits, a shock that brings a happy detachment. This is a break that, according to him, Chinese poetry often produces (and, I believe, all poetry worthy of the name; but Chinese poetry is especially close to the real). 'The more intense one's sense of the real, the less comprehensible it is,' he writes, quoting Clément Rosset.

Followed the entire ridge of the Vaux from south to north, all the way to Combe de Sauve. It was cloudy at first, then a strong rain fell during our descent. The leaves of the ash, still stuck together vertically in pairs, recall the valves of striated mussels, grey and light green, very beautiful from close up; the ash trees themselves, seen at a distance, create a silvery mass; the light where the old pines predominate also appears silvery, almost spectral. The oak trees still don't have any leaves at all. Under our feet, minute flowers of blue or white, unnamed. The clouds that had curled around the summits soon descend the slope behind us.

A hare dashes off and is immediately chased by the dog far into the valley. Because of its pyramid-shaped hills in successive planes under the falling rain, the bottom of the valley takes on a Chinese aspect. A few swallows shoot past overhead. Muddy water trickles along the paths, the mudstone is darker than ever. We skirt a grove of quince, the most beautiful fruit trees when they flower: Why?

Peter Handke in *Absence*:

> I believe in those places without fame or name, best characterized perhaps by the fact that nothing is there, while all around there is something . . . I am certain that those places, even if not physically trodden, become fruitful time and again through our decision to set out and our feeling for the journey. I shall not be rejuvenated there. We shall not drink the water of life there. We shall not be healed there. We shall simply have been there. [. . .] In that place, on the foundations of emptiness, we shall simply have seen the metamorphosis of things into what they are. [. . .] I need those places and—hear now a word seldom used by an old man—I long for them. And what does my longing want? Only to be appeased.[22]

Thus do we meet travelling companions in the too-often-desolate space of books.

Or predecessors, so precise and penetrating that one is tempted to give up following them. Coleridge, in particular, in his notebooks (those dated 1794–1808, the very years when Hölderlin wrote the bulk of his works):

When he compares melancholy to sunlight in a dying man's room, why does such a combination of words seem not only pertinent but even consoling in a way?

His note about horse dung echoing the cheerful traveller on foot in the morning frost is one that Issa, in his distant Orient could have written himself, precise and tonic as it is.

And, among so many other notes I would enjoy copying, this one, dated 1804: 'We are not inert in the Grave—St Paul's Corn in the ground proves this scripturally: Infants growing in their Sleep by natural analogy—What if our growth then be in proportion to the length & depth of Sleep—with what mysterious grandeur does not this Thought invest the Grave? How poor compared with this an immediate Paradise—'

Goethe, *Dichtung und Wahrheit*, Book XVIII. In the summer of 1775, when he's twenty-six years old, Goethe is already famous. He takes a trip to Switzerland with his friends, the Counts Stolberg, whom he deems, at least in retrospect, too exuberant and decides to escape their company as soon as he can. After a walk with a more sedate friend, Passavant, from Frankfurt, a future pastor, he returns with a poem about Lake Zurich, or two poems which he combines into one, 'Auf dem See'. The last two quatrains sound more or less like this (a large claim!):

> A thousand glittering stars float above the
>   waves,
> Soft mists drink in the towering horizon.
>
> Morning breezes envelop the shadowy bay
> And ripening fruit is mirrored in the water.

Who wouldn't think here of 'Half of Life', written by Hölderlin some twenty-five years later: 'With yellow pears / and wild roses everywhere / the shore hangs / in the lake'?

It's the 23rd of November. Because of Goethe, I'm rereading Paul Celan on Lenz. Furthermore, it's his birthday. He would be sixty-five years old.[23]

Goethe's poems, at least those before Weimar, are created in no particular order, without any plan for a book, day to day, and very varied: here a ballad, there a song, one to fit an occasion, then two or three odes, and all of a sudden, such a marvellous unclassifiable poems as the one about Lake Zurich called 'Autumn 1775', which again defies my powers of translation, although I'll still risk this miserable reflection of it:

> Verdis plus gras, feuillage,
> sur la treille qui grimpe
> à ma fenêtre,
> gonflez plus drus,
> grains jumeaux, mûrisses
> plus vite, et brillamment, plus denses,
> vous au'a couvés, du doux soleil
> le tout dernier regard, vous qu'emmurmure
> l'opulence nourrissante du ciel gracieux,
> vous qu'évente l'haleine
> magique de la lune,
> vous que ces pauvres yeux
> trempent comme rosée
> de leurs larmes en crue,
> les larmes de l'amour, source de vie[24]

Saw Ibsen's *A Doll's House* again on television. I believe Nora was one of Ludmilla Pitoëff's greatest roles. I've never forgotten her interpretation of Lumir in *Crusts* in Lausanne during the war. Because she was something else, something more than an actress: a soul on stage, the shudder of a soul illuminating this strange play. Which I am rereading. The first act is very good, fortunately devoid of the overuse of 'like' which sometimes weighs down Claudel's language. It's the emptiness of a world without God: 'I am surrounded only by the eternal rain' . . .

So I reread *The Humiliation of the Father* which follows it in the trilogy. All of Act I in the Roman garden, surrounded by the rustling of the trees and fountains, is a muted music that seems as admirable today as it did earlier. Act II is no less, not at all cloying or grandiloquent.

(It's not surprising if these pages remind me of another symphonist, Chateaubriand, invoking in his *Memoirs from Beyond the Tomb* a Roman feast that is quite real but stormier, the one he hosted in the gardens of the Villa Medici for the Grand Duchess Helen of Russia: 'I find it difficult to think of the autumn of my life when, in my soirées, I see passing before me those women of spring who disappear into the flowers, concerts and lights in my successive galleries like swans swimming towards radiant climates. To what delights are they headed? Some seek what they have loved already, others seek what they do not yet love. At the end of the road, they will fall into those sepulchres that are always open here, into those ancient sarcophagi that serve as basins for fountains hung on porticos; they will add to the light and charming dust. These tides of beauty, diamonds, flowers, and feathers flow past to the sound of Rossini's music that echoes and fades from one orchestra to the next.'[25]—And this, in turn, reminds me of the end of 'Hymn to a Divided People', which I knew by heart for a long time: 'And for a long time we heard nothing in the immense avenues save for the muffled rolling of a carriage, / And the distant dialogue of opposing orchestras at either end of the garden, / whose brass instruments the light wind strangely united than separated in turn.')

The contours of the ochre hills of Valaurie recall in places the famous *Chalk Hills on Rügen* by Caspar David Friedrich. Except, instead of opening onto the sea, they reign over the purple tillage like fire.

Angelus Silenius, German mystic poet born in Breslau in 1624. Roger Munier just published a selection of couplets from *The Cherubinic Wanderer*, the complete text of which he had previously brought out. Among the many I'm tempted to quote, just these few:

> You do not inhabit place, place is within thee.
> Cast place away, you will find eternity.

> The eternal word is born again today;
> Where? There where you are lost within
>   yourself.

> I wonder that you long for day so dearly!
> Never yet has the sun set for my soul.

> Friend, I have written enough. If you want to
>   read more, go hence,
> Become yourself the writing and the sense.[26]

The same brave publisher, Arfuyen, brings me, from a completely different place, the no-less-elevated voice of Buson:

> When mountain
> waters meet
> they fall silent

Also:

> At home
> how will I carry
> this limpid water[27]

(and I see that, despite the distance, these lines are much dearer to me . . .)

Goethe again. The very first version of *Wilhelm Meister*, in which Mignon is still occasionally presented as a boy, was only found in 1911. This unsympathetic, suffering character, who inspired some of Goethe's most beautiful poems, is an unusual invention and ill suited to the lighter side of his nature, the side the poet put forward most willingly. Mignon is an irreducible shadow in a mostly luminous landscape with an animal's untamedness, the exact opposite of Philine, who is also instinctual but carefree, cheerful, bright, casually pagan. There is a music to these female characters of Goethe which makes one think they could have been invented by or for Mozart; a dimension that wonderfully exceeds realism.

1989

Rereading *La Vita Nova*, written by Dante when he was twenty-seven, while thinking of my quince grove:

> As I rode out one day not long ago
> . . . I met Love
> in pilgrim's rags coming the other way.[28]

There is in these lines a beauty born of the limpidness that prefigures Racine—'The daylight is no more pure than the depths of my heart'—but with something more that might come from an archaic stiffness or from the youth that pervades his writing.

At a certain point, Dante notes that walking along a road bordered by 'a very clear stream', he was overcome with a powerful 'desire to compose poetry' and immediately thereafter the first words of the canzone 'Donne ch'avete intelletto d'amore' [Ladies, refined and sensitive in Love] came to him and he noted them 'with great delight'. As if it were the 'very clear stream' that induced him to speak and his speech itself imitated the stream, 'una riva molto chiaro'.

> Never should you, until death takes your sight
> forget our gracious lady who is dead
> So says my heart and afterwards it sighs.

This narrative constantly mentions people who are passing by, people whom we see passing, whom we hear speaking; there is perhaps nothing in the body of Western poetry as close to the most decanted music. What was necessary, sooner or later, was the appearance of pilgrims, passers-by by profession. It's the time of the Feast of St Veronica ('that season when many people go to see the blessed image that Jesus Christ left us as a copy of His most beautiful face (which my lady beholds in glory'): 'The pilgrims, it seemed to me, were going along very pensive and I, thinking of them, said to myself: "These pilgrims seem to come from distant parts, and I do not believe they have ever heard mention of this lady; they know nothing about her, but rather their thoughts are of other things than these; perhaps they are thinking of their friends far away, whom we do not know."' The motifs of distance, sorrow and passage seem to intersect as in a fugue. 'Then

I said to myself: "If I could detain them a while, I certainly would make them weep before they left this city,' and that is why he then writes the sonnet:

> Ah pilgrims, moving pensively along,
> thinking perhaps of things that are not here . . .

Other motifs in this crystalline counterpoint: eyes and mouths, smiles and tears, presence and absence.

MARCH

Today I realized that a line from Góngora came to mind when I was trying to define Jean-Pierre Lemaire's poetry which is of a comparable purity, if not mastery. Góngora's wrote his line—'Steps of a wandering pilgrim are these'—about the verses in his *Solitudes*, whereas Lemaire's lines are about an actual pilgrim of which a few still exist, even today:

> What the earth's sieve has retained
> on All Souls' Day, when the wind shakes it
> to release the year's ashes,
> still smoulders: the yellow and purple forest
> and your first heart, defenceless once again
> facing what it loves.

At the base of the lucid sky
he can present his offering to the altar again
and the Angel's stave rekindle the flame.

Andromache. How the name of an ancient heroine can condense within us, over time, with all the echoes other poets have given it later, even much later.

After Homer, even more, I believe, than the passages in which Homer presents her for the first time, it is Roud's few words that are most deeply etched in my affective memory: ' . . . and Virgil's Andromache created a paradise out of her sorrow'; upon which I had to reread Book III of the *Aeneid* with the arrival in Epirus where Andromache, now exiled, captive, had, as Delille writes, 'imitated all the things she mourned, Ilion, the Simois, the Xanthus, and through this sweet resemblance [she] deceived the sting of her losses.' A marvellous invention that Baudelaire, strangely, would take up in one of his Parisian pomes; and with that the verses, for me, approached pure magic:

'Andromache, I think of you! And of that narrow river . . . ' (in these lines I think I can now recognize that, without even knowing the rest, without even understanding, the mere connection Baudelaire draws in reverie between the word Andromache and the word river, of the female shade, exiled, melancholic, and the movement of the water, touched something very deep within me).

Rereading a collection by Jean-Michel Frank, *Music, Passionate Reason*. It has some very beautiful passages, which I have certainly not told him often enough. A Parisian brother of Schéhadé:

> Fatigue is an aspen, trembling in a hundred
>   breezes
> and chasing the turtledove's slumber
> to the shrubbery's smoother eyes
> the hawthorn stained with my blood
> the snowberry, a blind man's pupils.[29]

Pietro Citati is speaking about Kafka on television. It's striking that it was this miserable, neurotic man, this anxious mole of a man who preferred life over death, who wrote one of major works of our century—as if the century itself were ill. Was he a descendant of Hamlet, as Mallarmé so memorably pictured him, slender, dark, 'reading the book of himself'?

It must have been difficult for the other writers on the set with Citati, all of whom seemed comfortable with themselves, to talk about their books in this shadow—at once immense and fragile. But no, was my impression, not more than usual. It's true that it takes a lot to disconcert writers these days.

APRIL

From yourself, you will not draw much more than that
from yourself, that is to say, from this crumbling lamp
and from the flame that fades within . . .
. . . .
before going to rejoin those poor old bones
that no longer have either name or face outside your memory.

Dante, *Paradiso*.

For the record, quite simply, of all the passages that lift you high above yourself: it's in Canto XXVIII, when Beatrice explains the hierarchy of angels to Dante—which the poet would have found elucidated in the apocryphal texts from the fifth century attributed to Dionysius the Areopagite. The nine angelic orders are divided into three groups of three, which Dante calls *terne*; and of the second, he writes:

> The next Triad, which in like fashion puts
> forth leaves in this sempiternal spring, which
> the nocturnal Aries never ravages, is perpet-
> ually singing 'Hosannah' . . .

In the world below, our world, plants burgeon and
fade according to the movement of the constellation
of Aries the Ram, yet in the eternal springtime of the
higher world, plants escape its bite. These prodigious
lines should lead us back to the second *canzone* for the
'Lady of Stone', 'Io son venuto al punto de la rota':

> Leaves the power of the Ram engendered,
> to adorn the world, fulfil their hour,
> all the grass is dead, and all the green
> the foliage of all the trees lost to us,
> unless in laurel, in the pines or firs,
> or frozen in some other evergreen;
> so fierce and bitter is the season,
> it kills all the flowers of the field,
> that cannot tolerate the biting frost:[30]

More concisely stated, this metaphor in the *Paradiso*
is inscribed at heights to which I've occasionally
regretted that no Ponge seemed to aspire. (Why Ponge
here? Because of the long internal debate I had with
him when he wanted at all costs to place Malherbe
above Góngora and Shakespeare and, in particular,
making no mention of Dante; no doubt because he
didn't much like cathedrals . . .)

Italy. In Parma, the marvellous idyll painted by Correggio to decorate the deeply humanistic abbess Giovanna Piacenza's private quarters. In the museum, which has suffered an extravagant modernization —acrobatic catwalks of iron and glass, tubular scaffolding that serve no function other than a 'decorative' one—I'm captivated primarily by two remarkable statues by Antelami that came from the baptistery. A concert is being set up in the nearby Teatro Farnese; the harp is brought in to stage level through the window like a giant bird. The city is filled with air, space and charm.

Sunday night in Pavia, on the main square, not far from the pile of rocks that once was the campanile. Students are peacefully demonstrating for their fellow students in China. A lot of people are eating on the terraces, one is a young beauty with a dress so skin-tight, she seems almost naked. Then, like a Dantesque punishment, a cloud of mosquitos appears, so dense and so aggressive that most of the diners retreat indoors.

Of all the landscapes seen or rediscovered on this trip, I'd place none above those on the return journey, after Briançon, before Embrun, before Gap, those wide valleys; even more, the area between Serres and Nyons which had something simply sublime to it in the evening.

Dream. I want to undertake the ascent of Mont Blanc de Cheilon in Valais, which I picture again as a beautiful white dome (does this correspond to its real shape? I can't remember). The dream is interrupted when I'm cautiously advancing along a ledge that turns out to be a kind of cornice flanking the wall of a room; and my mother calls me from below—as if I were *verstiegen* (gone astray by climbing too high), to use the word from Thomas Mann's essay on Nietzsche, which I'd translated long ago. The return, in a dream, of this mountain's name, which I haven't thought of once since a childhood visit to one of my uncles in La Sage in the 1930s, is odd; but perhaps it's connected to the return to alpine landscapes I observed when annotating the recent reissue of *Requiem* and to the growing pleasure I've felt in the past few years when hiking at these elevations. As if an adolescent rejection of the world had given way, allowing me to return to childhood, beyond certain principles (in part theoretical, for that matter: the opposition of the sea, pagan, to the mountain, puritanical); as if impressions, more deeply imprinted in me than I realized, were finally rising to the surface.

Rather than going to contemplate the setting sun, red as it usually is in winter, it would be better to look at it between branches while clearing the brush. In the early cold, in strong wind, hands covered with scratches.

The polygonum's inverted cascade, that white abundance, weightless, that exuberance, although silent and calm, flowers raised on stalks or the wall, that foam, that cloud filled with bees. The common name is knotweed. That fits: it has what looks like a web of knots, like a foaming, buzzing snood.

While listening, on returning from a walk, to several of Brahms' intermezzos, it occurs to me that one of them is like knocking on a curtain of rain so that someone will come and open it. (Knocking on a curtain!— imprecise thought you have to seize and write down in passing; that, as a matter of fact, is how Brahms' music itself appears to me, rightly or wrongly, as having something a bit vague, which generally turns me away.)

From the beautiful volume of Yeats (in Yves Bonnefoy's translation), more than any other, I retain this short poem, 'Memory'.

> One had a lovely face,
> And two or three had charm,
> But charm and face were in vain
> Because the mountain grass
> Cannot but keep the form
> Where the mountain hare has lain.[31]

The *Letters from Switzerland* attributed to Werther, a work Goethe left unfinished, in which he wanted to show Werther before he met Lotte, are interrupted right after an account of an unusual adventure.

Werther, an amateur of art who is piqued that he has only ever felt unease at the sight of a Danae, declares that he wants to study the human figure as thoroughly as he has a cluster of grapes or a peach tree or a still life. So he invites his travelling companion to bathe in the lake—probably a memory of Goethe's swim in a waterfall outside Zurich with the brothers Stolberg, which had caused them a bit of trouble with the prudish Swiss police. The harmony of his companion's body exposed for the swim fills Werther with admiration; he believes he has surprised Narcissus contemplating himself in the spring.

'But unfortunately,' he continues, 'I cannot picture a Venus who holds him back, a Venus mourning his death . . . ' And so 'I resolved, cost what it will, to see the female form in the state in which I had seen my friend. We arrived in Geneva . . . ' It is there, in the city of Calvin, that Werther, posing as a painter, arranges with the help of a procuress to see, without being seen, female nudity for the first time in his life. Then, though he admits to his fictional correspondent that the image he glimpsed has enflamed his imagination and set his blood on fire, he also admits that nature, thus shorn of its veils, however gracefully done, struck him as 'strange' and almost horrifying.

Forêt de Saou. A basin defended by gates of stones, as peaceful as a cradle or a boat. The leaves of tall oaks fall slowly to the grass. Heather and scabiosa. At the base of steep hillsides, boulders and sparse grass.

The incredible verbiage that proliferates around works of art that are usually unworthy of the name; not surprising if young, fragile minds lose their way in it. A certain laxity of spirit leads to the careless use of language. If, at the same time, one reads Goethe's 'Alexis and Dora', or even the fragments of Ludwig

Hohl, the contrast is obviously enormous and offers food for thought.

From a volume of Goethe's *oeuvre* that covers the years 1791–97 (when he was in his forties), I especially remember those poems or passages from poems in ancient meters, in which much is expressed: flowers and fruits—or seasons, or moments—almost always tied to the most sensual love and yet bathing, at the same time, in a kind of expansive, admirable calm due to an acceptance of limits which coincides with the observance of the rules of classical prosody. A balance, to be sure, but one reached less through a decision of will or pretences than through maturation. So that it is all consonant, in the most natural fashion, to the point where even among the 'distichs', the intention of which is, at first, moral, one is tempted to retain several of them solely on grounds of their poetic merit. The summit that remains is 'Alexis and Dora', in which a garden becomes Eden again in an instant though the grace of art. As for oneself, in today's more dilapidated world, one might catch a few sparks of this fullness and glimpse a few of those golden fruits, those domestic suns beneath the leaves (and notably beneath the dark, gleaming leaves of the arbutus).

Life brings man fruit; but rarely does it hang
From the branch as red and gay as apples do.*

Or:

This time, oh Autumn, you sow only light,
  wilted leaves;
For this console me another time with fruit
  ready to burst.**

And these few verses from 'Alexis and Dora':
  ... you said tenderly to me
Take some fruit from this garden!
Take the ripest oranges, the pale figs; the sea
Does not bring you this fruit nor does any
  distant land.
And so I entered. You hurried to gather the
  fruit,
And the golden burden made your lifted
  apron swell.
How often I pleaded, enough! Yet even more
  beautiful fruits
Lightly touched, dropped into your hand ...

....

* Früchte bringet das Leben dem Mann; doch hangen sie selten
/ Rot und lustig am Zweig, wie uns ein Apfel begrüsst.

** Diesmal streust du, o Herbst, nur leichte, welkende Blätter; /
Gib mir ein andermal schwellene Früchte dafür.

And the final envoy:

> Now, Muses, enough! In vain you attempt to
>   portray
> How sorrow and joy alternate in a loving
>   heart.
> You cannot heal the wounds Love inflicts,
> But you are, gentle Muses, the only ones who
>   can soothe.[32]

After which, one should render a suitable translation of 'Euphrosyne', the wonderful elegy Goethe wrote in 1798 in memory of a young actress in the Weimar theatre who died at the age of nineteen.

NOVEMBER

I've read and reread much Giono over the past years; often with joy, so infectious are his pleasure and skill in storytelling. Fate decided that, having barely finished *Angelo*, I would see a show on television about the painter Bram van Velde, with whom I wasn't familiar and whose gravity, humility, slowness of speech, and silences were impressive. And so you're confronted with adventures that are almost incompatible yet equally able to evoke within you an admiring echo. Giono's insatiable appetite for life, for his subject and its vividness, on the one hand, and this emaciated old man with a bird-like face who says that the external world doesn't interest him and that all he seeks in painting, in sacrificing his life to painting, is to get close to a kind of model, an invisible figure. Given that, should you find yourself facing one of his works without knowing anything about the creator, then I believe you feel a kind of enchantment without the slightest tragic hue. There was, in what was shown on the screen, an extremely sensitive grace of colour; nothing at first sight to compare with works in which the difficulties of existence, suffering or despair has found form: like the late works of Goya, or Van Gogh, or Soutine. Listening to Bram van Velde, you nonetheless have the impression that you're discovering a painter alone in the world with his art, suspended by his art above the void, and about to sink into it should he ever let go of his paintbrushes.

1990

JANUARY

Henri Thomas. I opened my old, tattered copy of *Le Monde Absent* with exactly the same admiration I felt forty years ago (forty-three years—it seems unimaginable); more certain than ever of the perfection of several of these poems, which I would know by heart, if were I still capable of that.

> . . . golden words
> a timid voice
> pronounces at the edge
>
> of ageing forests
> give my life
> some shadow of meaning [33]

The Goncourts' *Journal*. A remarkable document about the Second Empire, about certain milieus they claimed to hate and depicted without complaisance but didn't stop frequenting. Avid for the eighteenth century, as was well known, they also had a feel for Rembrandt and Vermeer. But with regard to the art of their time, they place no one above Gavarni, loathe Ingres, dismiss Delacroix, and condemn the morbidity of Baudelaire; aside from that, they detest the seventeenth century and all ancient art. When they are moved, which is rare—by their maid's illness or by a pauper's face—it's their nerves rather than their hearts that are touched (as will be the case for Rilke in *Malte*). That said, they are master portraitists, virtuosi of the interior scene, in the manner of Hogarth; and occasionally, after all, their writing reveals traces of something that surpasses them or, more exactly, of moments when they surpass themselves: notably, when they describe their mistress asleep or an amorous reverie (like the night pavilion), or their account of the evening at the theatre which includes what they've seen on stage, in the seats, and backstage, and becomes, in their version, a wonderful allegory of human life. Ultimately, whatever the strange bounds of their taste and ideas, it's fascinating to see Flaubert, Banville, Gautier and Sainte-Beuve, not to mention all those extras on the Parisian scene who catch their eye, coming to life right before our eyes, all of whom they depict with extraordinary acuity.

If I were to retain only one passage from this teeming work, it would be the one in which we see

Baudelaire, sitting off to the side in the Café Riche as in Courbet's *The Painter's Studio*: 'Baudelaire is daydreaming at the next table, without a cravat, his shirt open at the neck, his head shaved, looking as if he were ready for the guillotine. With only one affection: his small hands carefully cleaned and manicured. The face of a madman, a voice as cutting as a blade. His pedantic elocution aims to mimic Saint-Just and hits the mark. He stubbornly denies, with a rather gruff passion, that his poetry has offended public morals.' This dates from October 1857, shortly after the trial for the *Fleurs du mal*. Another passage which reveals their antipathy even more clearly is from November 1863: 'People talked to us at the time about that street performer, Baudelaire, that he had taken a room off a corridor, always busy with travellers, a veritable train station of a hallway. He would leave his door wide open, to offer everyone the spectacle of himself at his desk, a view of genius at work, hands fumbling through his thoughts, behind the screen of his long white hair.'

A report, on television, about a bunch of conjurors and mediums now in vogue. There is a relation between their delusional bric-a-brac and bad poetry. There is also, at times, something ignoble and the limits of acceptable foolishness are widely overstepped.

Similarly, these days, when I stumble upon an authentic mystery in a text about a prairie in bloom, I take measure of how remote it is from these types of occultism (perhaps from more noble kinds as well); even if only for its absolute freshness.

I have just deciphered a poem by Emily Dickinson from 1859: to think it's contemporaneous with the parade of years I just watched passing in the *Journal* of the Goncourts! What a chasm between these two worlds! The Goncourts seem obsessed with the *putain*, the whore; this word and its synonyms in that period, is one that flows most often from their pen. It would perhaps be interesting to read that play (*Henriette Maréchal*) that inspires one of the strongest emotions in their lives when it was staged at the Comédie Française, booed, then had its run closed.

Listening to a Bach sonata for violin and harpsichord: the rapid movements progress like the conquest of a fortress or of the sky—rather the way the swallows in the Lance seemed to want to raise the sky in contagious jubilation. Could we say that the listening spirit advances in its turn towards something and that this something, paradoxically, is the forward movement itself? That would be like a hunt in which the capture becomes confused with the chase.

(To this I must add that Bach is occasionally a bit too martial a conqueror, too confident of victory; the militant texts are there for a reason.)

MARCH

On 18 February 1820, Keats writes to his friend Rice (he died a year later):

> Like poor Falstaff, though I do not babble, I think of green fields. I muse with the greatest affection on every flower I have known from my infancy. Their shapes and colours are as new to me as if I had just created them with a superhuman fancy. It is because they are connected with the most thoughtless and happiest moments of our Lives. I have seen foreign flowers in hothouses of the most beautiful nature, but I do not care a straw for them. The simple flowers of our spring are what I want to see again.[34]

The fig tree: its branches, in places, truly look like musical instruments, small green lyres.

JUNE

The marvellous letters written to Pasternak by Marina Tsvetaeva's daughter, Ariane Efron recall, in their bitterness and courage, Shalamov's *Kolyma Tales*. The horrifying absurdity of such fates defies reason. But there is an entire part of man that escapes reason.

Issa (1763–1827). I am reading, in German translation, the diary of his father's final days in 1801.

> Cherry tree in bloom:
> is there a single tree sheltered from
> the gamblers' quarrels?

But here is the funeral ceremony, the twenty-third day of the fifth month:

> Following the ancient custom, his ashes were gathered today at dawn. Everyone broke off their own stick from the deutzia bush and headed towards the cremation site. There, at this early hour, the last small clouds of smoke had already dissipated. What was left? The wind murmured sorrowfully in the pine trees. Before, on the eve of the third month, he had handed me the reunion cup and today, in this

breaking dawn, overcome with the grief of separation, I had to collect what remained of his white bones . . . [35]

> Spared by death:
> tears and the dew on the grasses
> now soak only me.

Beautiful weather. Last night, the moon's crescent appeared in the west between the branches of a tree, at a time when, lower down, the harvest could almost begin. That shadow, ours, of the earth, which only lets the thin orange crescent shine, inflamed, which creates this image—like a garment, a veil that reveals only a hint of a face or body and is all the more intense. Or like a letter that would be different from one night to the next.

Bracing heat. This morning, early, the cuckoo, very close to the house. And in the field below, wild chicory always lifting up its fragments of sky, its chalices— but that's not it . . . Church chandeliers? Listening devices, radars? Even less.

It's a plant that sticks up straight, that doesn't try to be graceful or even beautiful; it grows in a mundane way on the sides of roads and remains in bloom for a long time, as if it had a solidity that other flowers don't. It wears, simply, that shade of blue that discourages all approaches, all speech.

In fact, each of these plants is a kind of speech, borrowed from another language and whose closest equivalent might be the first salutation that rises one morning from the mouth of a child to the Virgin's feet.

Lying rigorously immobile across the path this morning, a very long snake the colour of pale jade seemed to me, as I skirted this obstacle at a respectful distance, to be a kind of phantom, a creature come from another world.

Surely, whichever path I choose to follow, whichever labyrinth I dare enter, if some Ariadne's thread is to get me out of it, it will be that of certain utterances, not necessarily grand ones, but clear, like the water of mountain streams. I drank from them with my child hands cupped in front of my mouth; I crossed them with a short leap of my child feet, on those slopes of sparse grass dotted with stones. They were so cold they seemed to burst from the mountain's snow-covered bosom, as in the *Lettera amorosa*: 'per sentieri di neve . . . ' If the thread doesn't break, I won't need anything more, today or later, 'nunc et in hora mortis nostrae'.

Reopening a notebook from August 1968 in which I'd jotted down a few notes on the events of May. Having followed them from a distance and as is my natural inclinations, I was grudging in my first judgement. Today, I only want to remember my reaction on reading the sixth issue of *L'Éphémère*, which appeared that summer.

I was struck by the fact that among the writers I most admired and still do, three writers from my generation, of whom two were editors of the journal (the two other editors, Bonnefoy and Picon had kept silent), René-Louis Des Forêts, André Du Bouchet, and Jacques Dupin, rather secretive writers whom I'd never seen engage in a political debate, greeted the events with equal fervour—a fervour I would probably not have shared, even on site: furthermore, each of them—very significantly—had believed he was seeing realized the very dream that fed their work, even if only for a few days: Des Forêts, an 'earth-shaking statement come, like truth, from the mouth of a child'; Du Bouchet, a new 'holiday'; Dupin, an 'uprising of signs' . . . These pages shook me at the time. I must have been vaguely ashamed of myself, for not being carried away by this wave of feverish hope. But I remembered, as I read that issue of the journal, that I'd happened on the account of Basho's journey, translated by René Sieffert, *La Sente étroite du bout du monde*, and I immediately said to myself, without another thought, that the narrow road is the only one I would want to follow without restraint, the only one I wouldn't stumble on. From the opening, from the very first 'stroke of the bow'—'Days and months are eternal travellers, as are the years that pass. Those who spend their lives in a boat or on horse until old age, voyaging day in day out, make the journey their home'—I was drawn in—'a scrap of cloud ceding to the wind's whim'[36]—ready, in this acceptance, to stop anywhere, to go in any direction, ready even for separation (the way one is drawn, so often, by that other, more melancholy kind of traveller that Schubert is). No revolt against the fathers here; instead, veneration for what in the past is pure, like the monument that survived a thousand years and, 'recalling the spirits of the ancients', brings tears to the traveller's eyes. In my eyes, such things could represent the pegs of a vast tent or the points of attachment of a spider's web (Joubert wrote that 'the world is made like a spider's web'). The absolute wonder of this prose, this poetry, is that it never stops weaving around us a web whose ties, always light, seem to offer us the only authentic liberty.

AUGUST

A first green leaf on the young fig tree spared by the fire appears like a new phoenix. More than ever, one is tempted to repeat after Silesius: 'God is the green of the fields.'

If I refocus my attention on what is truly important to me, perhaps I will find myself moved to limit my efforts to one last expression of praise, to a few more 'winged words' above and beyond all imaginable debates and all the labyrinths the spirit constructs. May these September days cross the internal sky like lucid herds, may late summer beat wings feathered with new green. Nothing more than this. Carried on this cool air, which, letting go of all that is arid and dead, prepares the resurrection. Counselled only by an open window and with my gaze directed at the white boundary between the last blue fields and the sky, at that flour, as if autumn's invisible master were a miller.

OCTOBER

Michel Leiris' last book, *À cor et à cri*, appeared in 1988. It's the 'frail sound' of a life's end, pathetic and tedious because he rehashes the same old complaints.

Ever more worn, the fabric of the text is coming apart at the seams instead of opening up to a brighter light or anything different. But reading these lines, almost the very last ones in this book, which will be his last: 'That there is, nonetheless, some poetry somewhere, that I might discover it in or introduce it into such beings, things, words, dreams, works of art, or books, changes absolutely nothing but instead offers a lesson it would profit me to learn. Indeed, I see this as a sign—at least in those happy moments when my irritable disposition loosens its hold—that all is not lost and that life evades the utter absurdity, the crushing idea of which haunts me';[37] reading these lines, I tell myself that I am, after all, hardly more advanced than he.

Claps of thunder, like the muffled collapse of rocks or breaking waves, well suited to my rereading of *Les Mégères de la mer*.

NOVEMBER

Rereading *The Idiot*. Aglaya's peals of 'radiant, fresh laughter' after a series of nightmares is, precisely, the torrent's irruption.

Sparse leaves in the tilled field, in the tilled earth, in bunches scattered by the southern wind.

A rainbow balanced on an empty house in a verdant combe.

DECEMBER

Maybe one day I'll have to admit that Beckett told the very truth about our times? Funereal clowning. Rereading him, I can't help but think of Kafka and the tenderness he inspires. Here, yet one more step is taken into darkness. But isn't there an extravagance that weakens the point? Hamm's exclamation in *Endgame*, 'You pollute the air!', expresses a deliberate rejection of the world that, to me, can only appear aberrant. The wall Clov is looking at is a wall that is even more wall than the one Hippolyte speaks of in *The Idiot*.

When Clov looks outside, he only sees that it's grey, not even night; the very worst: ashes. 'Infinite emptiness.' A kind of preconception of nothingness, with all the power and weakness of preconceptions.

Beautiful Chinese poems by the twelfth-century poet Li Qingzhao. Between these poems and the reader I am today, as so often before, time and space are almost irrelevant. It's our sorrow blended with the things of this world, with the day's movements. The ancient music that rises from a tearing, a rending.

> That the dust has collected on my toilet case . . .

Back from Dieulefit around four in the afternoon. On the steep banks of the lively river, in what little space there is left for them in the valley, green meadows with snow, freshly laundered sheets in the grass.

1991

On the Chenevis plateau: small, purple apples in the mud; and trunks of the old chestnut trees almost as baroque as the columns of St Peter's Baldachin.

'Obermann's Valley'. Having reservations about Liszt's music, I doubt I would have listened to the piece from his 'Years of Pilgrimage' with as well disposed an ear if it had a different title. I recently became aware of the sway certain words hold over me. (I didn't even know until yesterday if this actually referred to Senancour's Obermann or the name of a place.) There was, then, the word 'valley', which creates in me a sense of openness and movement, but alone it is too general to catch my attention. This was Obermann's valley, that is, a valley associated in my mind with Germany or German-speaking Switzerland, a valley through which Schubert's music might flow or his traveller might wander or perhaps the hero of Stifter's *Indian Summer*. A valley with a crystal clear waterfall and the waterfall's roar; bathing the grass and rocks—green and brown—in a *contre-jour*, a fog of brilliant light, and ahead of this, their steps. I'll listen to this work again; maybe it won't evoke these images at all and that would be just as well for the music. No matter. What counts for me are these images, this vaporization of the light that reached me from the horizon like an ancient call in which might be mixed a few scraps of memories from my childhood when I used to spend several days in the mountains—but that isn't essential. Despite Obermann, no melancholy tarnished its radiance. The verdant valley, the cradle bordered with rocks, watched over by snow, perhaps—or perhaps not if it's mid-summer and the mountains are just Prealps—the impulse towards the dazzling distance and to the traveller's right, like a staff of water to guide him, the waterfall happily led by the incline.

For this morning I'd like to note a verse from the epigraph Goethe composed in May 1785 for the Duke Leopold of Brunswick, who drowned in the Oder while taking part in rescue operations after a flood:

Ruhig schlummerst du nun beim stilleren
Rauschen der Urne . . .

(Now you sleep peacefully to the urn's quiet
murmur . . .)

❦

In his critique of Lavater's *Pontius Pilate* (1782),
Goethe expresses with admirable clarity the reasons
for his misgivings about those who are impassioned:

> This type of man 'regards what he is devoted
> to, the way those born rich view their wealth,
> as something that belongs to him, a given, a
> point of departure. But the object of his wishes
> and aspirations, that which he feels is lacking,
> which he believes necessary to enlarge and
> complete his existence, is what interests him
> the most and for this he will give up every-
> thing and will forget all the rest—a feeling
> that a third person, observing him, will not
> understand. When this sentiment takes hold
> of souls endowed with many great gifts, they
> abandon the vast internal domains of their
> existence and rejoice at the limits of their exis-
> tence, limits imposed on them as on all others.
> When they then attempt to speak or write
> about this, the result is often foolishness that

reminds us of our human world's constraints and we lament them even as those gifted souls believe they have experienced and revealed to others the most intimate, elevated, excellent, and profound aspects of their being.'[38]

About Kierkegaard, Shestov wrote in *Athens and Jerusalem*: 'If Kierkegaard had wished and been able to speak all of the truth, he would have had to root out from his soul all the ideas of "greatness" and of "knightliness" that his memory suggested to him. To one who had dedicated himself to faith there remains only "horror" . . . '[39]

Such was the encounter that occurred in my readings today; rather than an encounter, it was a collision of two irreconcilable positions, of the acceptance and the rejection of limits. And all this on a cloudy, rather gloomy January morning when the world is, yet again, on the brink of war. Goethe, anxious to exhaust the realm of the possible according to Pindar's old advice and probably because it suited him, and Shestov brandishing his anathema against all the docile, if not contemptible, emulators of Socrates, Spinoza and Hegel, in the name of the Bible and the absurd, and against Nietzsche and Kierkegaard themselves, whom he suspects of not having taken non-resignation to its limits, which is in his eyes the only chance of salvation. Goethe, alarmed by the 'excessive' who were appearing all around him: Kleist and Hölderlin, whom he considered mentally ill, no doubt all the more alarmed because he had not always been so different from them and their excess.*

It is obviously easier to follow Goethe's path than Shestov's. But perhaps there are better reasons for doing so? Even if the world's madness is so obvious today that it's more and more difficult to counter it with anything other than more madness.

....

* A significant document on the raptures to which Goethe could succumb in his earlier years is a few pages written in 1773 (he was twenty-four) on 'German architecture', which he dedicated to Erwin von Steinbach, the architect of the Strasbourg Cathedral, after seeing it: ' . . . Now then, excellent man, before I risk my mended boat on the ocean again, where I am more likely to find death than any profit, turn your eyes to this grove in which the names of my loved ones are still green. I will carve yours on a beech tree, tall and slender as one of your towers, and hang this handkerchief laden with gifts by its four corners. It is not unlike the cloth that descended, full of beasts clean and unclean, from the clouds to the Holy Apostle, full also of flowers, blossoms, leaves, and no doubt dried grass and moss along with mushrooms that sprang up over night—all of which I gathered as I walked through this region or that, botanizing to pass the time, and which I now dedicate to your honour until they decay' (Johann Wolfgang von Goethe, *Von deutscher Baukunst* [On German Architecture] [Sesenheim / Frankfurt: D. M. Ervini a Steinbach, 1773]).

Thus, I clearly see where Goethe and Hölderlin meet and even agree: where they are freely, exclusively and purely poets. There, all the world's poets speak more or less the same language.

Goethe again: the kinship of Mignon and Cherubino. Like Mozart, Goethe created a great variety of female characters, each as moving and charming as the next. Cherubino and Mignon are equally ambiguous; Philine and Zerline share a natural sensuality, full of tenderness and gaiety; Aurelie and Elvira are perhaps distant cousins. The marvellous beginning of *Wilhelm Meister's Apprenticeship* has the vivacity, slight madness and joy of a Mozart opera.

Very often these days, I hear with my inner ear a melody from *The Marriage of Figaro*, the aria Suzanne sings as she's waiting for Figaro in the garden at night—a veritable fountain of the clearest, most tender sounds possible. Perhaps it was having heard this aria—it's tempting to go so far as to say it was the only thing—that tore me from the darkness of Shestov? Having sensed it as the movement, the flow of water hollowing out the walls against which my head had been butting?

Listening to the 'Years of Pilgrimage', 'Beside a Spring': the imitation of the spring in music like the imitation of rain (Debussy), or fountains (Ravel), is unable to produce a freshness as pure as that melody of Mozart that doesn't pretend to imitate anything at all. Isn't there a bit too much imitation in such music? As much as the real world seems to me to be missing in abstract art, its echoes in music bother me; in 'La Mer', for example. It's important to be able to forget Debussy's unfortunate titles when listening to his music.

And so I listened again to 'Obermann's Valley'. For me, the beginning evoked terraces, a vast, open expanse in which the high and the low, the dark and the light are very much present. I also think of mountainous piles of sounds, of dark rocks, and of the title of Ungaretti's last poem. 'Petrified and Velvet', except that his velvet is not that of the prairies at the foot of the cliffs, but the female body 'that is so tender'.

Varèse, *Amériques*. Here, again, I'm bothered by the sense that it's too descriptive. I don't believe that the work's title is enough to make me see a superimposed image of skyscrapers and scenes from movies. On the other hand, as when I was listening to the 'Sacre' (but what am I going to write here?), I wonder if there isn't something superfluous in such displays of technique, in these studies of rhythm and especially of tone— considering the limited resources of classical musicians. Looking for extraordinary sounds, of course, and getting off the 'merry-go-round' as Ponge used to say, may be necessary, salubrious, exciting. But what if I'm satisfied with the 'merry-go-round', because it doesn't sound like one to me? I cannot defend against the feeling that the cost is excessive in relation to the results.

Before eight o'clock in the morning, the mountains are blue with veils of cold fog. It's the open enclosure, the crib, the combe where something is gathered; here, the mist, the earth's humid breath made visible by the morning chill. The beauty of the mist—always touching. When a mirror held up to a mouth no longer fogs up, it's death. The mud, the breath of the mud, in which today there may be some shards of glass, of ice, cracking underfoot.

Goethe in Italy: what strikes us today as too suave in a Guido Reni, or even sometimes in a Raphael, didn't bother him at all despite his love for the concrete, the real, the objective. It was probably his trait as a 'beautiful soul'. *Iphigenia* translates this very well.

And those two lines that may have been inspired by the landscape of Sicily in April 1787, in his sketch of a drama called *Nausikaa*:

> 'Only the nymphs on highest mountain peaks
> Rejoice in the weightless falling snow.'

Dream. At the end of a soirée, perhaps a family celebration in a large house—ours—located on a road through the centre of a village. The guests are leaving —it's still light out. I see my sister-in-law T., dragging her mattress behind her to load it into the car and I'm surprised she is strong enough. Then the cars start a bit further away. I'm taken with a young blond woman—or girl—and I whisper in her ear that once she has dropped off her friends, she could return, discreetly. She soon returns, but my mother is there and I know it would be better to conceal the start of this affair from her. We can't manage to and adapt to the situation by hiding all external signs of passion. From the front door, we look out at the countryside, a beautiful landscape with lush, rolling hills that resembles the landscape of my childhood more than this one. The weather is very fine, it could be a Sunday in summer. I suggest we go on an outing and the young woman agrees; but, realizing that she has an outing in a car in mind, I assume I'll have to induce her to walk. Then I notice an abnormally large man, a kind of giant, in a white shirt and trousers on a path that skirts a pasture. Two others soon join him. I understand that there's a circus there, though as soon as I've grasped this, the circus is, in fact, announced across from our house. I ask a horseback rider standing next to me in German when the show will begin. She answers in bad French, two or two and a half hours. Realizing that we're expected to attend, as are all the other residents of the village, and because of my mother, my companion and I are annoyed. A dark cloud forms over the house; rain threatens. Where, then, will they put on the show? I wake at that moment. Falling briefly back asleep, I decipher a rebus with certain symbols that should be translated by the word 'squadron', which confirms the dream's rustic, 'old-style' tone.

The girl, or young woman, did not resemble anyone I know. She was blond with a rather round face and of an indeterminate age, pretty, perhaps, but plain. There was nothing between us that evoked at any time passion, desire, or even tenderness; and yet, it was a love affair, hampered by the presence of my mother —a vague figure but, in any case, not very old. The hindrance of her presence was not, at any point, oppressive or forceful. I, myself, was not of any determinate age either; certainly older than the young woman but not by much.

What was striking about the dream is that it had a certain atmosphere from beginning to end—as do many dreams, now that I think about it. It was a placid atmosphere, pastoral, the atmosphere of a *ländler*, of the utmost blandness. A Schubertian dream, if you will, but not of Schubert at his greatest.

FEBRUARY

Walked in the snow to the farm on the Lance. A covey of partridges takes flight when we arrive. The paths are muddy in the valley, frozen higher up. On the way back, across from the cemetery chapel, those stones so like very old walls. A stone torsade frames the door like garlands of leaves in Greece for Easter; dense cypresses, nourished by the rare and very ancient dead.

At dawn, a yellow sun and a few sparse flakes falling lightly from who knows where, grey house flies.

Should I find it dispiriting or comforting to read today, 16 February 1991, these lines by Schiller, dated 1794: 'So we see the spirit of the time fluctuating between perverseness and brutality, between unnaturalness and mere Nature, between superstition and moral unbelief, and it is only the equilibrium of evils that still occasionally sets bounds to it.'[40] (This is in the fifth letter of *On the Aesthetic Education of Man*.)

MARCH

Mild weather. A walk first along a path mottled by the passage of a herd of sheep that remained unseen, then on that part of the path where many crocuses bloom right in its middle, lifting the soft, heavy earth like so many mauve lamps lit for the dead.

Coincidence. In his diary, in the entry dated 6 November 1910, Kafka mentions the presence of 'Consul Claudel' at a reception ('gleam in his eyes, which his broad face reflects'). With this he evokes 'a distant string orchestra' and 'in a loge, a woman with diamond earrings that give off almost constantly changing light': two important elements of the 'Hymn to a Divided People' ('And suddenly the flash of a diamond lights up the beautiful neck and small ear' and 'The distant dialogue of opposing orchestras at either end of the garden') from the 'Cantata for Three Voices', a poem that has always been particularly important to me.

The hawthorns, almost everywhere, the cherry trees, so much fine hail under a grey sky, this childhood celebration, strewn, spilt here and there, and there again, 'pure effervescence' (Hölderlin), a betrothal, how can you express it?

Dream. A doctor in L. telephones to prepare me for bad news about my old aunt H. (the one who, divorced young, consoled herself with a passion for chess). Indeed, I learn she has died. Later, a young girl takes away all that remains of her in a bowl; in the same way, and this is what I think in the dream, that I take the scraps left from dinner to throw out in the back of the garden.

Rosemary, hive of blue bees.

Music. Those 'rockets' I sometimes hear (last night, again, the wonderful modulations in Schubert's Sonata *Fantasie*) are utterly absent in contemporary music, it seems to me, even in that of a Debussy. Does this have anything to do with the 'death of God', the difficulty of using the word 'soul'? Does this correspond to the exclusion of the nude in painting, in which there is no longer any desirable feminine beauty after Renoir, Bonnard and Matisse? How was this lost? Why? Since we are still susceptible to it . . . Are we backward, are we survivors? Turning our backs to the future?

The unfolding of the linden's first leaves. And those of the fig tree against the morning light. The multiplicity, the luminosity, more yellow than green, the freshness of it all. The fig tree's leaves erect, the linden's drooping. They really do appear to be ignited; they transform the morning light into ornaments, light green fans, goblets. They shine like green water. They begin, they unfold, smooth out, unfurl, suspended from the branches or resting on them.

It's 1797. In their correspondence, Schiller and Goethe debate literary genres at length. At Easter, the first volume of Hölderlin's *Hyperion* was published and he is already planning his *Empedocles*. Schiller and especially Goethe regard him with suspicion, then forget him. In February, he had written a radiant letter to his friend Neuffer: 'She is as beautiful as an angel . . . '

Nearing death, one should be able to lean back against it, so as to see only the living.

Hesiod on the muses: ' . . . from there they go, wrapped in thick mist.'

Friedhelm Kemp showed me a passage from *Human, All Too Human*, entitled 'Et in Arcadia Ego', which expressed in 1878 with great density and power an experience around which many close to me have circled. If I had known of it earlier, I could have saved myself many laborious detours—this is, I have to admit, not entirely true . . . :

I looked down over waves of hills, through firs and pines solemn with age, to a milk-green lake; boulders of all sizes around me, the ground bright with flowers and grasses. A herd of cows moved, stretching and expanding before me; single cows and groups farther off, in the sharp evening light, near a forest of pine; others nearer and darker; all in the calm contentment of evening. The hour was half past five. The bull of the herd had stepped into the white, foaming brook and was following, now docilely, now with resistance, its tempestuous stream. He surely found in this some fierce pleasure. Two dark-tanned creatures of Bergamask origins tended the cattle, the girl dressed almost like a boy. To the left, rocky cliffs and fields of snow above broad swathes of woodlands; to the right, two enormous ice covered peaks, floating high above me in the misty veil of sunlight—everything large, silent and bright. The beauty of the whole made me shiver and impelled mute worship of the moment's revelation. Unthinkingly, as if nothing could be more natural, one pictured Greek heroes in this pure, vibrant world of light (without any trace of longing, expectation or looking to the future or the past), one felt as Poussin and his student must have felt it to be: at once heroic and idyllic.——Thus have certain men lived, have always felt themselves in the world and the world in themselves, among them one of the greatest men, the one who invented the heroic-idyllic form of philosophy: Epicurus.

MAY

In the notebooks for *The Idiot*, a few words scribbled onto the page——'Each blade of grass, each step, Christ' ——might hold the key for a response to Hippolyte's vehement nihilism.

JULY

The torrent, better even than the spring. Born of the mountain, suspended on rocks, carried high.

The end of Goethe's 'Amyntas' of 1797:

> Any extravagance is sweet! Oh let me enjoy
> the most beautiful all!
> Who, in love devoted, ever took counsel for
> his life?

Grenoble, *Museum of Fine Arts*. In these large rooms, where on looking more closely you discover a beautiful Lorrain and a beautiful Veronese, it is the four Zurbaráns that make the strongest impression, in part because they form a group and are of large dimensions. The big Rubens across the room seems declamatory.

Several things are captivating when you approach: an immobility, a silence, a near rigidity of the poses; the interiority, the reverence of a few figures and, naturally, of the Virgin; the monumentality—which had already struck me in Paris; but also a strangeness due, perhaps, to a few disparate details: the figure in the *Adoration of the Shepherds* who is pointing at Christ and looking at the viewer and who is much more realistic and rude, the heads on the left, behind the priest of *The Circumcision*, almost Goyaesque masks that are completely preposterous in this location, as is the impressive figure holding the candle, his face half-hidden under a red hood; or even the small attendant on the right, in the foreground, who also looks at us with a kind of wink and 'is almost nothing but paint'; or the kneeling king's hat in the foreground, the basket of eggs, the lamb with its feet bound together.

More profoundly: it's a power, an obvious fact, a rich and simple splendour, enclosed on itself— perhaps modern in that way—a candour of colour—

such that the mystery could be completely involuntary or the result of a lack of internal unity?

Next to the old, slightly dusty, high-ceilinged rooms, with pictures full of things and people, their dark varnish, their chiaroscuro, their heavy gold frames, you see the modern rooms open in parallel with very bare, white walls and paintings that range from a marvellous Matisse to works by the most recent painters, who it's not clear should still be called painters. The world's changes are strikingly obvious, as if summarized and proclaimed. In a certain way, you feel rejuvenated when you pass into these new rooms through the rediscovery of pure colour and the elimination of shadows as 'theatre'—sacred or profane.

NOVEMBER

On the Etruscan tombs in terracotta, seen again in the Louvre, the women often hold a fan. Death and lightness, frivolity, grace—death, and a puff of air to refresh a face already asleep, absent.

Two dreams of family dinners in which I am serving: uncles, aunts, all dead. As if I had taken several steps towards them.

Visited Henri Thomas: his gaze, at once concentrated and absent, all those lines by Baudelaire he knows by heart and quotes with delight, the questions he asks about them as if to himself; two large trunks that probably contain his manuscripts, a few books, naive Breton gouaches by Claudine Lecoq, for whom he gives me a letter—which he doesn't want to give to those 'darkies', the Haitian maids in what he calls his 'death ward'. His quiet humour, his profound sadness. He says, gravely, that he 'should have stayed'; that he hasn't yet learnt how to die, that no one has taught him (I noticed a similar confusion in Gustave Roud). He is brought a letter on pink paper, sealed: it's Gilberte Lambrichs writing him bad news about her husband: not something that will calm him down. He says that among those he still sees, there are 'people' and there are friends; the latter are few.

What a contrast, what distress next to the more or less noisy success of Sollers or Quignard who reign over the literary domain today!

DECEMBER

Walk above Bénivay. It's curious how often you find pieces of ammonites in the grey stones where ash trees grow, such that the fallen leaves, with their ribbing, seen from the grey side, constantly fool the eyes of those who believe they've spotted fossils.

A few crystals, too, like the remains of snow on these rocky slopes.

When we descend around five o'clock, the sun has disappeared, the stream, rather full, can suddenly be heard, a surprise. It's as if it's meant to happen when we come down, as if we were digging in the shadows to take out a spadeful of water—and forcefully. As if this freshness had burrowed into the trough of night or almost.

1992

Andrea C. died in a car accident the night of 29 to 30 December. Brought to the morgue in the hospice and laid on what is called the cold table. Not disfigured, but with a yellow-grey complexion. Horrible. The next day, again, in the open casket, which we are shown no doubt so that we can properly appreciate the carpenter's contribution to the funeral arrangement. The dead body is nothing more than an empty envelope. We cannot stay next to it more than a few moments.

I am looking at the detail from Giotto that Andrea had sent us a few days before she died. It's from the *Annunciation*: *The Angel Gabriel Sent by God* in the Scrovegni Chapel. A double-bay Gothic window, a white curtain suspended next to it with the end draped into the corner of this window, and behind it the blue

of the sky. This has a strange connection to this hor-
rible death, as if it were showing a shroud or, rather,
both an absence and an opening.

Already it seems as if the bud of the year were opening,
as if the sky were becoming wider and brighter.

Thought again of Andrea. Hollow days. It's worse
than finding yourself immersed in the fog again, or in
the long rains she hated. It's not 'worse' because
there's no comparison.

At Bec de Jus. Tall chestnut trees on the lightly sloping
fields. Rolls of fog descending into the valleys from
the north. There are traces of iron in the stone, the few
houses are covered with roses. Near some ruins, a rap-
tor gives a screech of alarm. We won't see it.

In Henri Thomas' last book, *La Joie de cette vie*—a
beautiful title for this survivor—I am moved by so
many phrases that are simple openings, at once lumi-
nous and sad, extraordinarily close to what might be

the best in me, but I would not have known how to formulate them:

> May you meet the eternity that loves you, men trembling before the mysteries of the age.

> There are voices like moments of fine weather behind the trees . . .

> Elsewhere, over there, those who are still living. The fires of my existence are subsiding, my farewells.[41]

On a day of intransigence, you could almost eliminate from your friends those whose movements of language don't speak.

A full moon in the east, but veiled with pink smoke. Behind this veil, suspended.

FEBRUARY

Céline in *Journey to the End of the Night*: 'Nobody can really resist music. You don't know what to do with your heart, you're glad to give it away. At the bottom of all music you have to hear the tune without notes, made just for us, the tune of Death.'[42]

Walser and Dhôtel, so close in their ingenuity.

MARCH

Dream. On a mountainside, rather high up, smoke is coming out of a corner of the forest. The beginning of a forest fire? As it spreads, some rocks not far from the centre explode with the heat and are projected all the way to where we're sitting in a car and I close the door so we won't be hit. Then birds, fleeing these altitudes, fly towards us. I see them where they've landed just behind us, large raptors. One of them has an eyespot, like a butterfly's, high up on his closed wing. They're much larger than is natural, almost as large as a man. Turning forward, I see another eagle approaching, flying just above the ground, accompanied by his mate and carrying before him his eaglet, its wings outspread.

Reread Gide's early work to finally have it clear in my mind. *Narcissus*, *Urien*, completely saturated with the moribund Symbolism of the day, are intolerably literary. But *Marshlands* avoids this weakness through liveliness, intelligence, cheerfulness and playfulness. Rereading this short book reminded me of M. P., whom our painter friend had christened Grégor, a gay pianist we would see out roaming every day at noon, inalterably stern and somehow absent, probably 'seeking whom he may devour'—but we had no idea at the time—who had told me to read it in 1944 or so. (His life, solitary and without much professional success must have been infinitely sad.) In discovering the book's date, a moment of vertigo: 1895! This novel will soon be 100 years old! It certainly wears the years well. At the time I'm recalling, Gide was still alive, very much a presence. The Belletrists, a society founded by students in Lausanne that was an accurate barometer of literary fads, had for a time sworn only by him. Then came Malraux. The turn of Sartre and Camus was approaching. There are still Belletrists in Lausanne, but I doubt they're enthralled by any masters of this kind today.

Fruits of the Earth was the gospel of a generation. Gide 'the poet' is execrable, even in prose. But I understand that this hymn to pleasure of all the senses has some power. It's clear that he's celebrating an intensely lived experience, even if he writes too much. Through it, we hear Nietzsche and, more unexpectedly, Rimbaud: a few echoes, unconscious, perhaps, but undeniable, of *A Season in Hell*. I think that Roud, even if he has only mild appreciation for Gide, would also have been sensitive to certain pages on the countryside.

With that, what literature of the privileged! Too many gardens, terraces, oases, far too many delicacies and too fragrant.

The southern face of the Mont Sainte-Victoire: a cathedral of stone, convulsively baroque, rising above the burnt fields.

Silvio d'Arzo's beautiful novella, *The House of Others*, of a nakedness and rough sobriety that is almost inconceivable in French literature today, almost always more psychological, elegant, 'of high society' or self-reflexive. Like Gide—rereading him, I finally grew tired of his writing, despite the perfection of his short novels, *Strait Is the Gate* and *The Pastoral Symphony*. As for *The Counterfeiters*, is it not unnecessarily complicated?

Malraux. The excessiveness of his persona at the end of his life, the sometimes confused inspiration of his books on art made me forget his strength as a novelist. The great dramatic scenes in which his protagonists confront violence, cruelty, death in *The Royal Way* or *Man's Fate* have lost none of their intensity. Of course, with him, we are closer to Beethoven than to Bach. But at least we've left the French gardens of Gide and his imitators.

JUNE

On the train to Munich, passing Lake Neuchâtel, the colour of steel: an excess of green all around and architecture that is paltry because lacking in meaning. Compared with the beautiful old houses in the last lakeside villages, they seem to herald the end of the world.

It's almost surprising to see wildflowers growing in this meticulously groomed setting: sage, poppies—I was similarly surprised when a siege of herons flew over our friends' little garden in Baarn in Holland. Poetry is on the side of these flowers, of these rocks, too, and cannot be on that of such inexistent and omnipresent architectures. This is not an expression of simple regret for a lost paradise.

A forest of fir, very tall, planted close together, trunks bare, with a shabby, pitiful air, as if they were desperately seeking air, higher and higher up.

German-Swiss women of a certain class and a certain age have large, rather noble face, delicate but severe. They don't dye their hair, use little make-up, have complexion coloured by the open air, and wear the elegant, sporting fashion of the English, dominated by greens and browns. I remember Mme R., the owner of Muzot.

In Zurich, waiting for the train on a platform right next to the street, I had time to watch a demonstration of young dropouts whose slogan 'Bäcki bleibt' (Bäcki stays)—the name of a city magistrate they want to stay in power—floats on a banner above a cart on which three musicians are playing. There aren't many of them and they're not at all aggressive. A man carries a young child on his shoulders. The police precede and follow the procession in cars. Officers are stationed along an avenue of trees: light blue uniforms, white helmets and small, round shields that look like they're made of wicker, extraordinarily Japanese in appearance. A flare speeds towards them, a few shouts. Then the procession moves on or disperses, out of view.

In the same station, when the train moves off, I notice right in the middle of the vast network of rails, a garden shack with a brand new Portuguese flag. The German train car is old and dirty, the velour seats worn and dusty.

Past St Gallen, I'm delighted to see the tall pear trees again that had struck me on my first trip. Along Lake Constance, the sky clears. A sign posted in the Rheineck station: 'Believe in the Saviour Jesus Christ.' Then Lindau, where I think of my mother for whom it was a childhood memory—a visit or a trip she had taken there—and of Montale's brief and beautiful poem 'Lindau' from 1932:

> The swallow brings back blades of grass,
> not wanting life to go.
> But at night, between the banks, the stagnant
> water wears down the stones.
> Under the smoking torches a few shadows
> still float off across the empty sand.
> In the open square, a saraband
> Churns to the lowing of the paddleboats.[43]

In Leutkirch, a pointed clock tower, another with a green onion dome. Only one person on the platform, short, plump, with very long black hair, maybe an Egyptian, then some children carrying dolls' suitcases.

Later, the train stops at Aichstetten—*ausnahmsweise* (as an exception), a voice from the loudspeaker informs us—to let off a group of hikers, almost as in the time of coaches. Germany certainly surprises me. It's finally warm, summerlike. Willowherb. We are still in Swabia. At seven o'clock, Memmingen. I drink revolting tea from a plastic cup, provided with a small wooden stick to stir the sugar. An old semaphore with arms like the ones we liked to have in our train sets, which have no longer been around for some time now. Many cyclists on the train. In Buchler a group of young Asian boards the train, and I wonder what they could be doing here: truly displaced persons, alas.

JULY

Thinking of the proliferation of colloquia, debates, and commentaries of all kinds: words that swarm and mill about like ants when a stick disturbs an anthill. The stick, the bludgeon of the end of the world?

ᔔ

Reread Christine Lavant's poetry in a selection edited by Thomas Bernhard: it's as beautiful as the old crucifixes in country churches, like old cloth, coarse and rough.

AUGUST

The bird that enters the forest on the other side of the field, in the shadow of the trees close together on the border: I don't know why it caught my attention.

Maybe it's not difficult to understand: it's that birds, especially relatively large ones, like the jay I saw, almost always fly free in open spaces. This bird almost seemed to be changing worlds, to be entering a kind of house, a green refuge.

Thought of Henri Thomas, of the postcard I sent him of a lekythos showing a young girl with a lyre.

Is it that the image of this image might help him?

Is it that no libation can quench the spirit in such places?

Could the image of the young girl or the image of the lyre in her hands,

or her presence, or her body so like a lyre succour the old man where he is?

Or is Morpheus' chemistry the only effective one?

Around three or four in the morning, a tawny owl cried. I hadn't heard any for a long time. The sky was lightly veiled, the stars dulled, it was still very hot.

SEPTEMBER

One dream among many, or, rather, a detail that seemed worth remembering. That death, I was told or I told myself in this dream full of various events, was the door I saw before me, the one mistake in the wall of a basement-like space, a massive, almost square door made of solid planks. I saw it open onto a second, similar door, perhaps covered with some climbing plants, like ivy, which did not open and surely never would.

Knotgrass, more profuse than ever, a sparse waterfall over the slope of its leaves, because the rain had pushed the clusters downward.

OCTOBER

The ritual emptying of the pool under rain so fine it can hardly even be called rain. You have to dig a small channel so the water will flow out without flooding the field of lavender. The water, at first the colour of pale earth, decants very quickly as long as you don't stick your spade in again. You see the bottom through something that is nothing more than a shining arrow indicating the direction of movement, that is almost nothing more than a fresh glitter of life.

Could you decant yourself like this, as long as you don't interfere and let the lustral water pour over you?

In this way we lived, wearing a coat of leaves;
then it gradually becomes tattered and ragged
but without impoverishing us . . .
Soon we will need only light.

Which words still have the right to be uttered in the ear of a dying man or even of one who is dying without hope of recovery? They must be the most appropriate, unquestionably, and without the slightest floridness (although the word is related to flower).

Isn't this the most serious question of all?

Keep the light. When your eyes begin to lose their sight or can only make out vague shapes or shadows, change the light to sound, make sounds that keep it radiant in your hearing. If you become deaf, make it travel through your fingertips like a spark. Consider that this body growing cold is fleeing in a flurry of wings an invisible figure of which birds are merely the turbulent reflections in our world.

Chanterelles growing in abundance, as never before, among the holm oak with mouldy branches, boxwood and holly oak: large splotches the colour of egg yolk, like dense flowers or spongy suns. They become more baroque as they age. The earth and the trees are saturated with humidity; the cold sky, pale blue.

The trees are turning yellow as if to compensate for the shortening days with more radiance.

NOVEMBER

A doctor, in an African folk tale, appears wearing a coat of leaves. This doesn't surprise me. I know several doctors clothed that way.

Gardening in dirt that sticks to my shoes. To the dark green of the acanthus, like a response at the end of the day, the pink and blue of the sky. The pink of the winter sky, the most faithful of all.

In the Fenollosa/Pound book on Noh I bought used in Mayence, the translation of certain plays I read as an adolescent in the 'Piazza Art Collection', now rid of the intolerable 'poeticisms', allows me to begin to better understand their power, as Blyth's edition did for me with haiku.

What captivates me most is the *Nishikigi* text,[44] a drama of unrequited love, in which a young woman who has rejected a young man's advances, represented by something the German translator identified as *Brokat-hölzer*, wooden sticks ornamented like brocade, tokens the suitor leaves on the threshold of the woman whose favour he's courting. There is a dense network of metaphors there, which I translated from the German version for the pleasure of it.

> We are intertwined like the grass pattern
> woven into this light cloth,
> like the voices of little crickets
> that live in skeins of dried seaweed.
> We no longer know
> where our tears have gone
> in the underbrush of this eternal wilderness
> . . . .

Narrow is the band of cloth from this loom,
but wild is the mountain river
that foams between the lovers,
between the man and the young woman.
The fabric they wove one day
has long since faded,
the thousandth night vigil
was for naught.

Later, the ghosts of the young people who died without having loved each other invoke the name of the wood sticks—*nishikigi*—and that of a narrow band of cloth with leaf patterns—*hosonuno*—that traditionally symbolize the suffering of impossible love:

MAN. These names are listed in the book of
      love
    every day until that year when three years
      have passed,
    the ornate sticks must be left here
    until they number a thousand.
    And the songs tell their stories today
    and will tell them in days to come.

WOMAN. These names are proverbial.
    Because the *hosonuno* cloth is of narrow
      weft,
    narrower than the weaver's breasts,
    that is what those women are called

whose breasts remain untouched by
>   man's hand.
It is a name in the book of love.

MAN. A sad name, indeed,
>   and sad to think upon.

WOMAN. A thousand brocade sticks have
>   been no use;
>   a sad name in a sad story.

MAN. Winged seed pods of the maple . . .
>   The seed withers and dies.
>   Never were we to meet.

. . . .

And later, the lovers' ghosts and the priest go looking
for the young man's grave and the chorus says:

All day long until dusk
we have trampled the high grass
on the overgrown road to Kefu
without reaching the cave.
You, over there, cutting grass on the slopes
where shall we find the way?
'You've no doubt asked for news of the dew
when frost covered this road . . .
Who is there will answer such questions?

The evocation of autumn that follows is marvellous (the Noh is one of Zeami's). Then, when the priest asks the couple to show him 'times fled / times buried under all this snow':

> WOMAN. The woman goes into the cave.
>   She sets up her loom
>   to weave the *hosonuno*, the cloth
>   as thin as the Virgin's son in autumn . . .
>
> MAN. But the suitor knocks on the barred gate
>   his hands full of brocade sticks . . .
>
> WOMAN. In olden days no answer came.
>   Not the slightest murmur through the
>   door, but only . . .
>
> MAN. The clicking of the loom.
>
> WOMAN. A sound as sweet as the crickets'
>   chirp
>   muffled like the voice of autumn.
>
> MAN. A sound heard night after night.
>
> (*They imitate the sound of the crickets.*)
>
> CHORUS. The cricket sews and sews his cloak,
>   weaves it out of prairie grass . . .
>   (*sound of the crickets*)
>   . . . like the whirring loom.

I retranslated all this as best I could since the dense network of references in these pages struck me as profound. It would be interesting to know to what extent this translation of a translation gives a sense of the original. A comparison of the Pound/Schmied version (the one I just translated) and the French translation by René Sieffert of another Noh drama, *Kakitsubata* (*Water Iris*), at the very least gives me pause. But one has to admit that the French translator's bias here discourages the reader.*

---

* The doubts expressed here were more than confirmed by the publication of a new collection of Noh dramas translated by Armen Godel, *La Lande des mortifications* (The Heath of Mortification), which contains the Noh drama I wrote about in a much more faithful translation—it's a remarkable edition—which offers the lay reader a much more abrupt and enigmatic text.

Here we have, then, a splendid example of the game of telephone: the Japanese original, a Japanese-style English version of the original by Fenollosa, an English adaptation of this version by Ezra Pound, a German translation of this adaptation, and finally my French version—lightly sketched out!—of this German translation! [With the added dimension here of my translation of Jaccottet's French version into English, of course. —Trans.] We can assume that Pound, after Fenollosa, has 'Westernized' the original by making it more explicit or, at least, by making the connections more visible even it means inventing occasionally or, indeed, misleading the reader. My concern, complete incompetent that I am, is not to judge. It is certainly possible that what touched me so deeply is not in the original, notably, for example, the passage I quoted about the search for the cave— the tomb—with the mowers who, when asked the way, answer ironically as if the question were absurd. Let's be honest, I would

Mayence. In Germany, where modern construction is frequently—much more than elsewhere—massive, square and dull, the presence of Baroque or Rococo architecture is disconcerting. There no sense of connection between it and the modern construction, of course, but there's no connection with people's lifestyle either—in contrast to Italy where city life is expansive, exuberant and therefore suited to the whorls, the effusions, the splendour of stone or stucco. The disparity is all the more obvious because everything here has been renovated, made impeccable, licked clean.

Most of the passers-by seem of modest circumstances. No trace of luxury to be seen.

Twice I have a sense of uneasiness. At the sight of a child who, having escaped his mother at a bus

----

probably not have been as moved by Armen Godel's version, which to all appearances is simply exact and in which we are told in a note that two earlier poems are cited in this passage in a system of echoes characteristic of the art of Noh, to appreciate which, you must be well read in Japanese literature.

Therefore, I should, strictly speaking, have crossed out these few pages. Still, the essence of what I wanted to say is not there. As the Portuguese proverb quoted by Claudel for the epigraph of *The Satin Slipper* says: 'God writes straight with crooked lines.' Sometimes mistakes and approximations can be fruitful. (1994)

stop, runs along the platform muttering and sobbing. His expression, at once brutish and unhappy, and the anxiety of the mother chasing after him, probably worried about the embankment so close to the river. And at the sight of the pale invalid with a gaunt face who steered his wheelchair with a violent gesture up to the table in the tea room where I was having lunch: a doleful, aggressive Jew, who is anticipating the return of Nazism in the near future and claims he wants to buy two cars specially designed for the handicapped and then emigrate to the United States. He is obviously angry with the entire world. I believe it was a long sentence in prison on political grounds that made him an invalid.

1993

FEBRUARY

Montaigne on cannibals in Book 1 of the *Essays*: what a lesson in tolerance and intelligence with America only just discovered! No doubt he idealizes these 'barbarians' in contrasting as he does—well before Rousseau—their closeness to nature, their naturalness, to our artificiality. But the sentences full of irony with which Montaigne concludes this essay in which he had tried to show how very little barbarity there was, in fact, in the customs of tribes he is discussing: 'All this is not so bad, but what of that? They don't even wear breeches.' It should be engraved in the minds of all racists these days. (I heard almost the exact equivalent from the mouth of a young Frenchman back from Algeria at the time of the 'events': What do you expect of those people? They don't even know how to tie a tie!')

In *Elective Affinities*, the passage from Ottilie's journal after visiting the chapel she decorated with the young architect:

> Whatever it is we're doing, we always conceive of ourselves as seeing. I believe men dream only so as to not stop seeing. Perhaps some day the inner light will shine out from within us so that we won't need any other.
>
> The year is ending. The wind blows over the stubble and finds nothing to sway; only the red berries on those tall trees seem to want to remind us of something more alive, just as the beat of the thresher's blows reminds us of how much life and nourishment lie hidden in the grain that has fallen under the sickle.[45]

The thoughts that occupy the beginning of Part Two in the novel harmonize with that cold afternoon in Avignon on which Jean Tortel was buried. We would rather have seen him returned to the earth in the garden that was his true place for so many years instead of being stacked in one of those stone wardrobes that are family vaults. There were fewer people than I'd expected. Jeannette all of a sudden bore the full weight of her age, which she had seemed miraculously to escape for so long.

I must have some kind of mechanism of immunity, which kicks in under such circumstances without my even wanting it and prevents reality from sinking in. This hardly seems laudable. I see without really looking: I have no taste for funerals, not even with flowers. Might as well remember that last visit, not so long ago, when Jean Tortel, even much weakened, was still completely himself, radiating friendship as few are able to do with such constancy.

Along the hillside road to Aures, bordered with grey stones so uniform they look like walls, a few violets among the dark boxwood; and on the northern slope, the last traces of snow.

APRIL

On the north face of Mount Linceuil. The raw green of the pastures is the shade of the large, green lizard, the one Dante refers to as *ramarro*, as I learnt when translating Montale's 'motets' with Luciano Erba, in which one of them darts out like an arrow.

Passing Curnier, a lovely, compact village away from the road, I noticed another pasture next to the river. Why? There were no animals there, no children playing, and yet it wasn't empty. I think that once again, because the river was so close, the light dwelt there in such a pure, tender way that it became a kind of promise.

Dream. My wife and I are to meet my father on Île de Ré, but we're very anxious, not knowing how to get there. The dream's atmosphere is odd because of the sense of profound helplessness that saturates it. In a dark station—night is about to fall—a train of only First Class carriages has stopped at the platform. The travellers are all worldly people or, at least, wealthy ones, which perhaps explains why we hesitate to board so long that we finally watch it pull away under our noses.

Then high, snow-covered mountains by the sea appear, as if we were in Norway, which surprises us, since we're still trying to reach Île de Ré. We find ourselves in a kind of cavernous concrete hall, waiting in a queue, but before us is the opening of some sort of tunnel intended for a cable car and we understand that skiers are waiting to get to the top of some run. At this point, in fact, I notice skiers arriving at the bottom of the run—there is no sunlight—one at a leisurely pace, the other at full speed. I tell myself that I surely can't do the same and, in any case, that's not how we'll get to the island, where my father must be running out of patience.

I vaguely remember another scene with long wooden tables set outdoors on a square—maybe still in the middle of or not far from docks or hangars. Servers wash the tables after having cleared them and I wonder if my mother was present in that scene. A heavy sadness weighed over it all because of our father, waiting for us in vain.

Fine weather in the garden and the images of the world we see broadcast and rendered banal on television: unbearable. Wounded soldiers in Tel Aviv, one of whom resembles Quasimodo, blind pilots playing ball, a little girl, anesthetized and with teeth that are too long, like an animal's. Another day, the blind Bosnian child right after our prime minister's utterly sleek pronouncements.

Images of the SS and Jews in the Warsaw ghetto, the former cutting the latters' sidelocks and laughing: the mocking of Christ. And the absolute, vile horror of hate. There will be no end.

Questions, like arrows, like swarms of arrows; maybe one and the same question.

Rumi in the *Mystical Odes*: 'Leaves, like missives, carry green signs.' Or: 'Words are this wind that once was water. They will return to water after throwing off their mask.'

Rereading what I wrote about the Maddalena Pass, I think: this is nothing but a soap bubble made of words; as long as we are outside it, we think it is real and lasting. Is it something more than an iridescent bubble?

(But when Rumi wrote 'Eternal life shines on the leaves in the garden,' there were probably no fewer intolerable events happening around him than there are today around any poet who has begun to doubt the reality of light and the legitimacy of the word, to the point where he blushes at being called a poet.)

An extremely thin, sharp crescent moon—and the absolutely pure white of a few blossoms, half-closed, of the dog rose, like two rhymes.

Crystal fishhook.

Italy. Poster for an exhibition of an 'abstract ceramicist': *Profili del pensiero*, no less!

Near San Giuliano Terme we are held up for a long time at a crossing near a large agricultural hanger that has been turned into a 'Scarpe in' shoe shop (does that mean you can select your shoes without getting out of your car?) and dance school, under a large magnolia.

Sienna. Walking along the Piccolomini palace, you inevitably recall the verses of Du Bellay: 'more than Rome's audacious facades'. What pride, what confidence presumes such dimensions! But this excess doesn't create a sense of emptiness as so many others do. These days the marvellous shell of the Campo, like the Spanish Steps in Rome, draws human wrecks whose laxity is the opposite of what made its conception and construction possible. A recorder plays inanely on one side.

Castello di Gargonza: this village, described in 1974 by the TCI guide *Toscana* as a 'minisculo borgo semi spopolato, di alta e solitaria suggestione' is now a 'charming area'.

In Torgiano we meet Inger Christensen, the great Danish poet, still extraordinarily placid in appearance: a peasant woman at market. But her art is an elevated science of words.

At breakfast, Hermann Lenz recites a charming poem by Ronsard to Anne-Marie, though not without difficulty since he hasn't spoken French for a long time. He tells us he how he came across the poem during the war in the forest of Fontainebleau, a real Eugen Rapp story—his novelistic double. The poem, a celebration of the good life ('Buy me apricots / Melons, artichokes / Strawberries and cream: / That's what I like in summer / when, beside a stream . . . ') fits with the sumptuous banquet we are offered.

JULY

Dream. I have to go to Kornfeld or Krefeld in Germany, probably to give a talk, and I ask where this place is. I'm told it's in the north, in a sad, industrial region. The dream immediately offers me an illustration: an enormous factory, half-obsolete, which I compare, for someone who is with me (I don't know why), to a huge, rusting ship and I'm rather pleased with the aptness of the comparison. An almost empty building.

Two or three labourers are still working on scaffolding (I see them from a distance), when a man (or maybe two) armed with a knife, attacks them to shake them down. The scene changes: now, an enormous crowd has gathered, shoulder to shoulder, in the factory, all wearing the same outfit made from a kind of brown burlap bag—it might recall the crowds of Masons, and on waking it will remind me, in its size and number, of *Metropolis*. But the atmosphere is much darker, oppressive, wretched and especially 'more real'. The man with the knife is still there and still threatening, threatening me as well with his blade.

A little later he will end up in a kind of massive wooden cage that looks rather like an elevator cage. But he's not entirely captive, one of his limbs has been crushed under the weight of this machine—which is as simple and frightening as an old instrument of torture, an extraordinarily rough and heavy contraption. Overcome with pity, I think, I help him free himself. So through me, he escapes punishment, and in me, regret replaces fear.

We call these dreams, but there is a part of reality to which these dreams are infinitely closer than my life is.

Wild chicory: a blue that is always truly celestial—for a Fra Angelico of the fields. They are gaining ground along the rising road, where we hadn't seen any until now. But they only open in the morning. In the afternoon, it's as if they had disappeared. The blue of the children of Mary. Bound to the morning sun. If the latter is too present, too close, they close—as we close our eyes.

Yesterday, the ballet of three buzzards in the twilight sky, their sharp whistles and the thin crescent of the moon.

This morning, the same three buzzards salute the sun at dawn across the way, above the water tower. Where the thin dyer's plumeless saw-wort still blooms, slender on stiff stalks, with pink, hirsute tufts.

AUGUST

Dream. In a German city where we had gathered for some literary conference, there are low houses lining a canal. Since I, alone, ventured a bit farther, I find an almost deserted neighbourhood with a very tall, beautiful church—as tall as the one in Trani, but bigger. Then I find myself on some terraces or bastions, with a few other people, one of whom calls my first name in a loud voice. They are soldiers or Customs officers. There's a barrier, a control post. I'm told, in German, that I've wandered into a forbidden zone. The anxiety that is in so many dreams takes hold because I realize that I'm very far from the hotel and I've even forgotten its name, which keeps me from resorting to a taxi. At that point, someone helpful wants to show me where we are on a map, but the map is old and we can't manage to unfold it. It's much too big. I don't know if, in the end, it is any help or not, but my anxiety grows as more time passes without my being sure I'll find my way back.

Later, I'm on the edge of the canal, therefore, on the right path. A.-M. is with me now, along with another woman, I don't know who. In a long covered pool, probably a large washhouse, an old woman is swimming and she waves her fist at us. This fist is a bloody stump. I think she's insulting us.

(It could be that I was influenced by reading Nerval that very afternoon, especially 'The Severed Hand' and 'October Nights', in which we meet old madams in dim hovels.) The scene on the bastions was nerve-racking but beautiful. The ending was horrible.

Deeply moved by my rereading of Nerval. The musical melancholy, a lightness that sometimes gives you shivers; the naturalness of the diction, its suppleness, its liberty. A singular magic:

> Where are our past loves?
> They are now in the grave.
> They are happier there
> In a more beautiful place.

(Let's forget my praise, in the first edition, of an imagined version . . .) Or the poem that starts with 'Already, the fine days, the dust', like lines by Henri Thomas, like those of Thomas' early poems I like so much.

SEPTEMBER

Mild and calm afternoon. Emptied the pool.

The braids of water, the ones we can easily unbind. Several autumns in a row, I've written lines about this.

I also thought of Shalamov again who, returned from the last circle of hell, the one of the permafrost, the eternal ice, has only one idea: to write poetry again. That should sweep away our scruples. The man who survived the worst needs the clearest language. Don't forget this.

Poetic language, he writes still in the camp, is my fortress in winter.

In the middle of the night, I thought of adding at the very end of the last text in my book:

 . . . Thus does the old poet climb back on his high horse . . .

    It seems to me that he's not wrong (that he saw something clearly from up there, etc.) . . .

    but (I'm trying to reconstruct what seemed convincing in the middle of the night, but hardly is now) I prefer to watch the clear water at my feet stream into the ground,

    the last braids you'd like to unbind . . .

And may what follows make no more noise (than the water that disappears down the slope).

What remains of a recent dream that was meant to be taking place in Russia, the impression of having been someone lost, if not suspicious, there, but accepted in the end by the natives—a young couple with children—who spoke Italian, which allowed for reassurance, for a relatively familiar exchange. But even odder, before this encounter, an image: bees rising and falling like Cartesian divers in the middle of a small glass cage, giving me, in the dream I believe, a very comforting sense of warmth. It was as if I were being given a sign in all this greyness and cold. I said to myself, still in the dream or when remembering it on waking, that the bees were like the tungsten filament in an incandescent light bulb. Their yellow colour must have been very intense, their waists rather like those of hornets.

OCTOBER

On Edgar Morin's *L'Esprit du temps*. He is very concerned to distinguish himself from certain intellectuals who bemoan the decline of culture. Very well. But when he mentions the 'striking analogy' between Homer's heroes and those in the popular press, it would be nice if, simply for the sake of rigour, he then said a few words about the abyss that separates them. The same goes for the ancient gods and those he calls the 'new Olympians': movie stars and celebrities. Many agree with his analyses because they are so apposite and, too worried about being taken for a nostalgic intellectual, he even goes so far as refusing to judge. It's remarkable that one of the rare occasions on which he loses his level-headedness is when he writes: 'Mass culture poses a fundamental problem. This is not the problem of its artistic value. Setting Debussy against Louis Armstrong is insufficient, ridiculous. Setting Montaigne against Dean Martin, Socrates against Jerry Lewis is inane.'[46] On the contrary, that is the entire problem, the problem of the considerable distance that separates the sculptures of Roman porticos from comic strips and Montaigne from Dean Martin. If he only lets irritation show on this occasion, isn't that significant? It's as if one were pretending to deny any difference in altitude between Mount Everest and the Buttes-Chaumont.

Rereading the beginning of the Old Testament, in Dhorme's translation, my first reaction is a completely naive astonishment at the idea that in Europe almost everyone's childhood was fed by these stories that originated in a practically Oriental country, a country of deserts and oases, of farmers and nomadic herders, a country of sand and harsh sun, where wells are the most important meeting place. Whereas most of us have only known forests, lakes, fog and bleak winters, which should have made us more susceptible to Scandanavian, Celtic or Germanic legends. But these stories, as a result, had the charm, the prestige, the lure of the foreign and perhaps that drew us to them more readily?

The cherubim were winged bulls like those guarding the entrances of Assyrian palaces: the devaluation of words.

There is, in more than one episode, the same naive, native force as in Homer: Sarah and Abraham's laughter when they are granted their belated son, whom they name Isaac ('he will laugh'); the story of Sodom with the surprising mob of citizens impatient to see the three angels staying in Lot's house; or the nocturnal scene of incest with his daughters (which was the subject of the painting in the Louvre by Lucas de Leyde that I found so striking long ago).

The name Lebanon means white: moon.

Esau's trick recalls Ulysses escaping Polyphemus: stories of shepherds. How they like tricks, almost all of them! Roman sculpture seems to me to have marvellously reinterpreted this world in visible figures.

And so we were asked to obey a God, Yahweh, who, having chosen one people to serve him, ordered them to exterminate, in the most radical sense of the word, all those who resisted in the countries they conquered. Is there any compatibility at all between this God and the God of Christ? It seems that theology thinks so. And how can one not understand contemporary Israelis who want to rule a country whose borders are so precisely delineated in the Bible and who are also assured it will be theirs for all eternity? How can they be cured of certitudes that today are aberrant?

Those great songs, like Deborah's, one of the oldest biblical poems, fuelled by the intoxication of victory, not say carnage.

What a beautiful book Paul de Roux's *La Halte obscure* (The Obscure Stop) is! Like the 'Ménandre en avril' (Menander in April):

> You reading Menander on a bench,
> you are more obscure than this Greek text . . .[47]

Fig tree turning yellow, losing one by one its leaves so like and so unlike hands. The noise of the dried leaves on the flagstones, a slight noise, like elytrons or bark. Under the rapid glide of white and pink clouds, when the cold begins to fog the windows. Like age fogs the gaze, extinguishes the eyes. ('You look much better today,' the doctor said sympathetically to my mother-in-law as if he could not see, next to the window, her waxen face gaunt with the fatigue of too long a life.)

Evergreen trees are a much darker green than the others, a blackish green. Taller than the others, straighter, they're almost the colour of night. You could think of them as old warriors or ancestors as straight as their sceptres or bludgeons.

The noise of dried leaves, a slight, brusque noise, a thin murmur, as if they had no more flesh, no more thickness or suppleness. Light, brittle, starting to shrivel—because detached from their roots. Jacks with which the wind plays carelessly on the flagstone checkerboard. Old men with brittle bones, dull eyes.

Burnt letters, therefore words that have burnt. Strange distinction between the paper on which they'd been written, which blackens, bursts into flames, and disappears into a bit of ash and ash-coloured smoke—but some fall and others dissipate into the air—and these signs that burn in a different way.

ॐ

What may still be worth the trouble: a few brief words
without any vibrato.

NOVEMBER

Those words I still dream of confusedly had been
found by the monk Saigyo in the twelfth century:

> Could this be the place
> Where I lived
> long ago?
> Moonlight glitters
> on the mugwort's dew.

Or this poem of winter:

> We may regret,
> yet even the bell
> has a different sound,
> and now frost has replaced
> the morning dew.

Or this question for after death:

> At that time,
> on my pillow

under the mugwort's roots,
will I still hear
the insects' intimate chirp?

Tomas Tranströmer. Since I first met him in Trieste
in 1989, a stroke has left him almost completely unable
to speak and with difficulty walking, but he still comes
to the Petrarch Prize ceremonies, his smile illuminated
with kindness, distant but not as distant as all that. His
few poems translated into French by Jacques Outin
are marvellous. 'Schubertiana', for example:

And the man who catches the signals from a
    whole life in a few ordinary chords for
    five strings,
who makes a river flow through the eye of a
    needle
is a stout young gentleman from Vienna . . . [48]

That led me to listen again to Schnabel's recording of
the 'Impromptus': the D. 935, No. 1 feels like cloth,
like fabric with its grain, like fur, material of sound
rather than sight. The D. 899, No. 3 takes me back
to the effort I made at the end of my last book to cap-
ture this strange and distant rustle of fabric—fabric,
there again, at its most ethereal. Yet to express this or
nothing about such marvels . . .

Montélimar–Geneva by train, 2 November. In Cruas, the smoke, fog and high water of the Rhone: a phantom landscape. The sun doesn't return until we reach the Isère River. There, for an instant, a true Millet or Daubigny painting emerges: cows and carts under the poplar trees in a light so frail, it seems elusive, hardly real. Then, still bathed in this fragile light, to the left, beyond Grenoble, a mountain shaped like a truncated pyramid, a veritable sacred monument built in another world. And on Lake Bourget, perfectly calm and shining in the sun, a fisherman in his boat is doubled by his reflection like a king on a playing card.

An idea that has pursued me for a very long time, that a certain part of the 'Song of Songs' as transposed by St John of the Cross is one of the highest points ever attained in poetry. Like those peaks in a mountain range that remain illuminated after all the others.

Having had to reread the only collection of Lamartine's poetry I had available for a theatre project organized by some friends, I am at first put off by the length, the excessive fluidity and eloquence of many of the poems, convinced that this verse is no longer readable today. Then I come upon the beginning of 'Thoughts of the Dead', which my daughter learnt at school:

> See the leaves without sap
> As they fall onto the grass . . .

because of this, I rediscovered them with delight. It seems nothing inspired Lamartine more than time's acceleration when we feel it racing towards death or night. He then achieves a transparency close to that of Racine, more diffuse, more elegiac and less controlled, to be sure, but still admirable.

> The water no longer charms
> The forest with its murmur;
> Under the leafless branches
> The birds have lost their voices . . .

This lead me to read out loud the whole of 'The Vine and the House', which also filled me with admiration. In the melancholy return to childhood, on the threshold of death, he seems to turn in towards his centre and rise to his highest level; then as happens in Hugo's writing, though surely in a more virile way, his eloquence ceases sounding hollow. Yet once again, it's the rapid movement of his octosyllabic line that I find most convincing.

Lively gleaners of November,
The thrushes on the mourning vines,
Have forgot the amber clusters
Young, we would covet with our eyes.

DECEMBER

In the fog this morning, the pigeons' flight above the
road: they are the colour of pale ashes, ghosts of birds
almost.

1994

Continuing to read Ronsard sonnet by sonnet: what a different effect than with my exploration of Blyth's anthology more than thirty years ago in which each haiku, or just about, day after day, revived me because they gave me back the world and almost my breath. Now, despite the sparse beauties in this or that poem, I have to force myself to continue. The poet of haiku was first a sage—or a lunatic. Ronsard is first an artist, driven by the ambition of being the best poet of his age, and of equalling or surpassing his ancient models.

Reading Martin de Gard's *Journal* plunges me back into a world already distant but which I frequented when I arrived in Paris, where the word 'Vaneau' had the power of a talisman (it was, I think it is now relevant to remind others, the street on which Gide lived). I reread, at the same time, his *Confidence africaine*

(African Secret), a remarkable narrative, and *Un Taciturne* (A Taciturn Man), two works that clearly reveal what their author was most interested in: characters obsessed with being restrained because he himself had, secretly, very little restraint. It seems, in the end, that what counted most in his life, even more than his *oeuvre*, was the familial knot, the family drama. What a waste for someone who claimed to be horrified by any and all passion!

North of Sainte-Jalle, mostly arid slopes, rather bleak, with veritable lodes of grey ammonite, a few ravines in which quite strong water flows—because the ground remains moist—with traces of passing herds: their wool caught on thorny gorse bushes. Almost too much silence and emptiness in all this, and cool weather. On a hill with a cross, a shepherd's dogs come to bark at us, then welcome us—as if we were the only distraction of their long Sunday. They come from a farm, half-ruined, almost a wretched encampment.

The children in Sarajevo who held an invisible string stretched taut over an icy road to trip passers-by, the others who got out their sleds: the life force.

In the place called 'the large meadows' this morning someone lit a fire in the muddy earth of his garden. This smoke suddenly speaks to me, though it may be a shred of fog lingering here. The man standing next to it takes a large step back.

MARCH

Dream. Clouds hover before me, the colour of ink, not unlike the spots in Zao Wou-ki's wash drawings in front of a landscape that otherwise appears extremely sunny. It's a hillside of sliding earth, almost mud, on which I'm afraid my mother, who is walking next to me, will slip. This does, in fact, happen. A fall, probably not serious, but I remember seeing her bare ankle, which perhaps I rub (an image that may have come from the previous evening when an elderly friend showed our hostess a spot he had on his leg). In any case, since we had been walking in this warm-coloured dirt with the consistency of clay, we have to wash off our feet in a nearby stream of a clarity in the bright sun that seems fantastic, almost poignant.

Then I see a young relative stretched out on his deathbed or in a coffin—with nothing sinister or distressing about the sight. He props himself up on an elbow, like an Etruscan funerary statue, opens his eyes, asks if there's a door open somewhere, and goes back to sleep.

The passage in *Conversations of Goethe with Johann Peter Eckermann* that concerns a young man who writes to Goethe, who was over seventy at the time, to ask for the outline of the second part of *Faust* so that he can finish it himself and this leads to a critique of presumptuous young authors and the spirit of the times, which proves, once again, that the sentiment of decadence is nothing new. ('Professional bunglers will multiply . . . ')

APRIL

Noted in *Poèmes de tous les jours* (Everyday Poems), a selection of Japanese poems from all periods:

> Oh, cherry blossom! Fall in clouds so thick
> That age loses its way.
>
> (Ninth century)

> In the field under the snow the grasses have
>   been effaced
> The white heron hides itself in its own
>   appearance.
>
> (Thirteenth century, Dogen, Zen monk)

Morning shadow, I am no more than a
    shadow of myself
For having seen the pale brilliance of this
    pure jewel unfold.[49]

(The commentary on this poem by Kakinomoto no Hitomaro, who died around 710, explains that the pure jewel is a female figure.)

The extraordinary and aggressive ugliness of the decors in television shows with which almost everyone is saturated: all of a sudden, we wonder if there has ever been the like before. Could we conclude that there is no ugliness in the living environments of populations that are still more or less archaic? The clothing, the objects, the décor in the huts, in the caves, they all look attractive to us: Is it an illusion? Closer to us, in the seventeenth century, Versailles was surely beautiful, but so were the farms, the peasants' furniture and cutlery, however wretched their circumstances. Is this idealizing the past? Sometimes you see, in newspapers or in books, architecture of the poor of staggering beauty. I remember seeing painted interiors, in North Africa if I'm not mistaken, that were as beautiful as a Matisse or a Miró, breathtakingly beautiful. Might ugliness (in this domain) have only begun in the nineteenth century with industrialization? And might it be a sign, among so many others, of an onset of agony?

What a few of us are still writing has no place in that world. That's why we must be subsidized, protected, supported like the last churches, the last ruins—out of compassion or a guilty conscience?

From the very beautiful Book VII of *The Republic*, this passage:

> Last of all he will be able to see the sun, and not mere reflections of him in the water, but he will see him in his own proper place, and not in another; and he will contemplate him as he is.

Later, in Book IX, on the tyranny of Eros when given free rein as in dreams:

> [T]he point which I desire to note is that in all of us, even in good men, there is a lawless wild-beast nature, which peers out in sleep . . . But now that he is under the dominion of love, he becomes always and in waking reality what he was then very rarely and in a dream only; he will commit the foulest murder . . .

In Book X, on the punishment of tyrants when spirits 'bound them hand and foot and threw them down, and dragged them along at the side of the road, lacerating them and carding them like wool . . . ' [50] You could be reading Dante, who no doubt was familiar with these pages.

An abundance of irises in bloom. When you're at their height, it's a little like swimming in their midst, that is to say, that when there is such a profusion of them, they make you think of water more than sky, although 'think' is not the right word. A visual sensation of water, moreover a rather vague one because water hardly is this colour and water moves and shines more. Maybe it's their transparency that brings these flowers so close to water, because it is certain that the marigolds at their feet are completely opaque, even solid—staying close to the ground. What is unique about the irises is that they are held aloft, atop their stem—like topmasts, like hanging pavilions—which lends them a particular lightness. (You could, as in so many other cases, develop them into a highly refined figure because they are complicated, elegant, heavily perfumed flowers, very feminine. But, also as in so many other cases, you would only discover their external truth, a false magic or an inferior one, as happened to me with the peonies, not being able to get any further except after the end of text.) The feeling of water, an immediate and confused sensation, is probably the most precise: matutinal water—like the feeling you get from distant mountains illuminated from behind in summer. You're tempted to thank them for this water, for this refreshing draught; for this summer morning.

It's in the shade, the shade of the linden, of the fig tree, that irises give the sensation of water, of watery coolness, most vividly. In the sun, they fade and wane.

MAY

Finally read *The Words*, which I'd never opened before, having come upon it by chance in a friend's library. A remarkable book, certainly, but how can anyone be so interested in himself? Or is it I who am strange for having never interrogated myself this way?

There's more room to breathe in Nabokov's memoirs, a more than privileged child of old Russia, because you're not trapped in a 'psyche'. That world, in which one had fifty servants and the lady of the house *never* went into the kitchen; on the other hand, she would go pick mushrooms in the woods.

Dream. It begins, as I recall, with a large fish swimming in a basin at my feet—my daughter is next to me, perhaps some friends, too. The fish grows larger and more threatening as it rises to the surface. I see a maw with teeth. It aggressively bites my foot, but I manage to free myself. Then there's a visit, guided by a child, of a strange place with a chapel, no one understands what it's for. Then an enormous city where we can't find each other again since we hadn't agreed on a meeting place for whenever we get separated (I don't know who this 'we' is, except that my mother and father were part of the group). The anxiety grows as the day draws to an end, with the worry that we won't find an open hotel, not having any way to reach the others, who, in the end, may only be my mother. As if the dream wanted to remind me how 'lost' she had been at the end of her life, how impossible it is for me today to be with her again.

Listened to Bach's 'Motets' yesterday, marvellous, and Mozart's 'Quintet for Piano and Winds', no less marvellous, but in a different way. All these 'proofs' I'm thinking of because of a new interview I am preparing in connection with my most recent book, these things that are also real and that banish despair, that absolutely must be said again, then, just as what you have touched and seen in the mountains must be expressed: the water's wing. Things to stiffen the spine. The sarcophagus-like fountains I mention in a note appended to *Requiem*. Their tinkling heard long ago and rediscovered now. And Mallarmé's verses:

> Voice foreign to the wood,
> or without echo, a bird
> that not more than once would,
> in any lifetime, be heard.

After these lines in Mallarmé's poem, there is a fall, like that of Icarus, the punishment for those who would fly too high. But if it's true that we cannot always live in exaltation, the fall may not be deadly. It doesn't mean that the flight, the exaltation, was a mistake or wrong. Or else it would be as if the mountain climber, having reached the summit and returned to the flatlands, were to deny that the peak continued to be one.

The flatlands are the (mental) landscape through which Jean-Christophe Bailly, in his remarkable short book, *Adieu*, invites us to walk from this point on, turning our backs to the mountains, home of gods who have disappeared for good. But the mountains don't only crush—just as the Christianity he has in mind didn't just forbid, suppress and suffocate. Sometimes, behind us, they illuminate the flatlands we are crossing.

The dog rose, once again, about which I surely won't manage to say anything that I have not tried to express already: white, pink, even salmon, with their golden centres, their perfect simplicity, their fragility—the child, the little girl, the angel, perhaps.

That they build delicate arches that rise and fall and that they are gracefulness itself, rustic. Particularly moving on the rocks, where they adorn, as bushes, the dark ruins of oaks burnt in a forest fire—like the hand of a young girl resting on very old stones; in the forum of oak trees.

Or if they climb in the foliage of an almost black holm oak—as I've noted already about a cypress tree—perfect stele and the most desirable—the rise of grace around the funerary columns or simply obscure columns—without noise or weight or depth—like a rondo?—or like the pairs of butterflies in spring flying ever higher?

The first fruits of summer: the golden greenery, the length of evening, the return of the swifts that no longer are, for me, a fisherwoman's hooks or the points of arrows. I have forever left the beautiful theatre of *The Solitudes*. Deprived of this target, sheltered from these sharp points. It is not only for the good.

It's now hardly possible to rise at dawn. Does this mean you have little chance of reaching eternity, of passing through the final gate? or is this just a game of words without guarantees?

Perfumes exhaled by plants that have no other voice. Honeysuckle, privet. For the bees.

Whistles, swifts tirelessly rocketing past in squadrons. Black as cast iron, like cast-iron tools. Practically without feet.

Readings for Pentecost: the sound of a mighty wind that announces or accompanies the wonder of the tongues of fire. The Holy Spirit as breath and as flame, which allows for universal comprehension. We are wide of the mark today. Almost everywhere fire does little more than destroy.

JUNE

Afternoon heat. The sky almost incandescent just above the rooftops, light blue higher up, where even the swifts appear calmer, less greedy, almost always taking time to glide.

Valente's *Landscape with Yellow Birds*. I sometimes have to struggle to enter this work that is so denuded as I do with the works of Juarroz or Jabès. The lines for the dead son that give the collection its title help:

> I thought I knew one of your names that would bring you to me. I didn't know it or couldn't find it. I am the one who is dead and has forgotten, I tell myself, your secret.

Or on the following page:

> A man bears the ashes of a dead person in a little bundle under his arm. It's raining. No one is around. It seems like he is taking his package somewhere.

What makes this page throb is certainly the 'little bundle'. These words, that thing, are necessary to keep everything from dissolving into an abstract whiteness.

Valente grabs a tenuous thread, a most tenuous thread, but one that suffices: 'I am right on the edge, a thin rim of non-existent shade.'[51]

The dog rose is already almost done. Brief, then, and frail in its jumble of thorns. Why is this plant called 'dog rose'? I don't know. The word *églantier* comes from *acus* or needle via *aquilentum*. My parents had a servant named Églantine, of whom we were very fond. They continued to see her until her death because she passed away before they did. She had a face as round and pink as an apple. She was slender and warm. She had married a very thin postman with sharp features, who could easily be compared to a crow. His demeanour was as funereal as Églantine's was gay, pleasant and spring-like.

This has nothing to do with these flowers, which we hardly have enough time to glimpse and praise. Childlike. Childlike garb for the trees, for the underbrush. And completely wild. Wellsprings of roses.

I walk to Ventabren along the base of the hill, covered with aphyllantes, broom and daisies in bloom. The last of these, since I'm thinking of dog roses as I pass them, are completely different although the same colour or nearly. A bit stupid, a bit flat, as opaque as little plates with the yolk of an egg in the centre, a bit stiff, too. You'd think certain flowers would 'open onto' something else and that others would be mute or closed. All this is really not serious.

Dog rose blossoms: short-lived and fragile, a currency that is not valid for long, nonetheless, an image of the only obol valid for passing to the other shore? The only one you cannot hold tight in your fist where it would wilt immediately; nor can you hoard it. It would be as if, one day, you heard something murmured or simply spoken some distance away, as you were passing through some place. You could even imagine a man condemned to death walking towards the place of execution, whom such a sign—which he will grasp almost without turning his head—would allow to advance without weakening.

This white that is not a dead, sanitized, opaque white, nor even in the slightest bit cold. I see very well that in pursuing it with my thoughts, I'm risking slipping into reverie and finding the flowers of the almond, the quince, the cherry trees, of which I've already been only too solicitous. But what is different is the absence of any link to future fruit, filled with flavour and substance for us. It's absolute savagery, liberty, thorns—and the combination with other trees, equally wild, on which the dog rose blooms. Ornament and savagery. All that, says nothing about them.

In *La Piedra y el centro* by Valente, this note: 'We looked, we saw the ultimate radicalness of our poetic language in Góngora. It's in St John of the Cross that we must seek it—without prejudice for the Cordovan's poetic grandeur.' One must read the essay later in the book entitled 'The Eye of Water', in which he evokes the connection between water and night, that river, that bottomless body of water, which, according to the 'Song of the Soul', no one is able to ford 'even though it is night'.

JULY

In *The Knight of the Cart* by Chrétien de Troyes, the comb the queen forgets on the edge of the spring—as if the only thing left to comb were water. Amber, absence. Amber and pure water. Such regions, as in the preceding note, are the ones through which I like to roam.

❧

The song of the warbler is imperceptible in the trees even though they are very close.

❧

That beautiful medieval word 'reverdie'.

AUGUST

Dream. My memory of it begins with the presence of D., the peasant who sells lavender oil. He invites me to his home and before we go, he asks that his wine be brought. What should have been a case of bottles becomes in the dream some kind of large, flexible palisade of corrugated cardboard, taller than a man, which requires the help of one of wine merchant's employees to carry. I look at this more-than-cumbersome parcel with astonishment, wondering how the bottles are arranged in it, if there really are bottles. Now and then I try to help with the transport. (It was about as awkward as carrying a mattress.)

Then, without transition, I find myself walking alone along the bottom of a valley that ascends towards a high rock wall, a landscape that recalls certain Gauguin paintings of Brittany and is so beautiful I promise myself I'll return in good company. At one moment, turning around, I notice below white spots among the stone walls and trees and I realize, with a kind of exaltation, that it is a herd—of sheep or goats, I no longer remember which. But I also note that my vision is blurry, even with binoculars, that I don't see anything very clearly. I am, in addition, absurdly burdened, carrying a package (again!) in my arms and a woven straw basket.

Later, and higher up on the slope, after hesitating over which path to follow at a crossroads of faint trails in the purple or dark brown dirt, a little old peasant woman who looks like a Noh witch passes me, walking at a brisk pace. I admire her agility, while she certainly looks significantly older than I am, compliment her and overtake her. She then replies that, if she's not mistaken, we will arrive at the same goal at the same time, all the same (the kind of thing we say in our minds to a driver who pointlessly passes us on the road into a city to which we are both headed).

What was remarkable in this dream was the breath-taking beauty of the Piedmontese landscape with its strong, though muted, colours on the one hand—and on the other, my handicaps: blurry vision and arms filled with useless things. It would be too easy to read it as a moral fable.

Pink morning glories in the vines at ground level: these little chalices, this tender colour, as if barely emerged and distinct from the earth. These fragile seals on the secret of the world.

OCTOBER

Don't forget the dyer's plumeless saw-wort that kept me company while I gardened in September, as did a robin close by. A slightly hirsute flower and frail, despite its rigid stalk, a particularly modest presence, pink and wild, which fills you with delight although you don't know why. Almost nothing, which the hand of the weeder spares as if it were a rare and precious thing. Last summer's companion, along with the bee-eaters concealing their colours and their liquid cries—as if they were drinking as they flew—or like winged wellsprings, mobile and gay.

Dreams, *in Florence*. In one, a child reputed to be dangerous appears and bites a woman I don't know and all this in the naive and occasionally cruel style of certain predellas by Fra Angelico. In another, I'm watching strange, large birds, semi-transparent, half-grasshopper, half-vulture. It's like seeing skeletons covered in plastic wrap. They come dangerously close to us, hiding beneath some trees.—I no longer know who this 'us' was. After this I see a procession of spectral people and I remark, even in the dream, that they perhaps belong to another dimension of the world.

Other dreams, *in Bologna*. While we are hunting for a thief with two policemen who are driving our car, we have to go through a pass that is so narrow the car body gets scratched even though I asked the driver to be careful. Beyond it, we find a very primitive farm on a steep slope and, behind it, a hovel, in which the policemen are sure the thief is hiding. Indeed, the thief appears: a very poor, old woman. Right when the policeman are about to apprehend her, I notice a very tall peasant standing in the field that looks as primitive as his farm. A cleaver—or a billhook—gleams with a hard light at his feet. He grabs it, splits one of the policemen's heads very neatly, and then starts towards me—terror wakes me immediately.

(You can see martyred saints with a cleaver in their heads in certain paintings, but I haven't seen any lately. Instead, I do remember a recent crime committed with a butcher's cleaver.)

In the following dream, at the same time we're hearing that Delhi is burning, I see an entire expanse of countryside overrun with animals fleeing the fire, running in my direction.

It rains hard all night; our window looks onto the side of the cathedral, which has beautiful medallion sculptures.

'The cold season.' It could be a title. Nothing that burns, nothing that devours. As when we leave, and naturally it's the case, whether we like it or not. Nevertheless, the world is still there; the foliage shines; the light on the morning horizon is a white haze. The spider webs are also shining in the window, fragile and tenacious—exemplary in this. There is no way to feign 'perfect joy'.

The fragrance of mint leaves in a child's hand: this is one you breathe, at once close enough to touch and so removed, in the cold that falls after sunset, taking you by surprise, the cold of imminent winter.

If I were to transcribe one more time on this October date: 'Lovely Sunday walk . . . path lined with flag-stones and walnut trees . . . ', etc., better not to write anything at all, or I will be the first to tire of these rep-etitions, the first to worry about their futility 'in times of distress'. And yet, 'do not keep for yourself what you have received . . . ' There are places that improve you when you walk in them, even if only briefly. The insignificant little valley behind La Paillette is one. Maybe the trunk and bare branches of the walnut trees, relatively rare in these parts, answered in their silvery way the colour of the flagstones and, with them, pro-duced a particular, almost antique, light. At the same time, the sound of a rushing stream so abundant it cre-ated small waterfalls here and there, combined with the tender thickness of the grass and its different kind of abundance in the meadow along the path formed together an accord of energy and rest, of conquest and welcome, almost joyful and limpid nuptials; while, higher up, other tree essences would already be changing colour, would be igniting under the sky's grey humidity.

Same thing, elsewhere—this time near Montjoyer on a plateau covered with garrigue, a wild combe called Malecombe, prickly with ochre-coloured rocks, like a fortress that is at once heroic and immemorial, the earth's bone, here as if stained by an ancient fire, looming up amid hirsute vegetation—reminding me of Poussin's momentous paintings in his final years, *Orion*, *Hercules and Cacus*, in which the rocks and the heroes, or demi-gods can not be told apart.

NOVEMBER

Tall poplars like spindles from which fall leaves of gold, coins; spindles that are unravelling. It occurs without a sound, without any tearing, more like a bestowing, as if time were distributing gold coins; or as if one were releasing one's final poems, one's very last, luminous pages—in those combes where there is almost always mud and water.

I think of Góngora: 'Green sisters of that auda-
cious young man,' of that marvellous sonnet that
evokes, after Ovid, the metamorphosis of the Heliades,
Phaëthon's sisters. 'The bark reached her face at these
final words. Their tears still flow, dripping from the
young boughs, these drops of amber, hardened in the
sun are caught by the clear stream and carried to the
young women of Rome to wear as finery' (Ovid).
Beautiful fabric of fables, of lies if you will, that
nonetheless encompasses a tangible truth, leaves car-
ried on the water, tears as adornment.

The spacious and golden light of evening, bare
branches and certain shades of purple, cold half-moon,
cloud-coloured—an echo, when I raise my eyes, of
my rereading of Leopardi's 'Memories'. The way we,
all of us, have re-experienced these emotions, almost
exactly the same, though no doubt in a manner less
absolute and also less cruel, emotions I cannot tran-
scend any more than I can erase them from my being
or keep them from returning.

> Ogni giorno sereno, ogni goder ch'io sento,
> Dico: Nerina or più non gode; il campi,
> L'aria non mira . . . [52]

No other poet knew how to extract clarity from sadness as well as Leopardi. Perhaps what was necessary was the Italian language brought to its pitch of perfection?

More enchanted steps at the foot of Mont d'Autuche. The light is intense, as always after the mistral has swept away the clouds and rains. It's already warm on the southern slope even if the paths are still muddy. At its base we see a small valley strongly illuminated by the afternoon sun—descending towards Condorcet. Initially, it's a ravine, wild and dark, then it opens onto green fields, onto well-ordered orchards like the fine stands of oaks in the Hölderlin poem, and finally, in the distance, a narrow river gleams. One of us exclaims that this is 'like paradise'; fortunately, I'm not the one, being too accustomed to such excesses not to be the first to distrust them. And yet, after all, there should be a beginning of sense to it! Usually, it is in dreams that we are granted such vistas, views that bring tears of astonishment, of gratitude, of joy to our eyes. A hunter has caught up with us: his son and a friend are hunting snipe a bit higher up. We hear two gunshots; they've killed one of them. Even though he doesn't look a day over fifty, has good posture and a fine bearing, he repeats the exact same phrases three or four times over a short span of time: that, having hunted all his life, he would prefer, from this point on, to follow the path and let the young ones beat the brush; and those young ones, you have to explain everything to them . . . He insists that he's confident there's another snipe in the area. We discuss their rarity, their price, the one we let hang, which then stank so awfully, we—oh sacrilege—threw it out of the window for a passing dog. The sun shines down on these words, too.

But none of this explains the kind of 'transport' such views induce without any change to our condition of being mortal nonentities. It seems to me that no alchemist will ever create a finer gold than that with which this place and this moment seem to be not so much impregnated as winged. It's like a transfiguration in which nothing of the material figure is lost because everything we see opening up before us still bears no other name than tree, forest, earth, plants and water.

There is, thus, among the multitude of pages written ever since man invented writing, a few pages structured in such a way, written with such ink, that they produce in us analogous transports.

On one of the hills lit by the setting sun, it's impossible to say if what crowns it is a band of rocks or ramparts.

Liszt's last works for piano in Alfred Brendel's fine interpretation: truly deserving the designation of 'lugubrious', 'funereal', the first translating just with its verbal sonority something of theirs. All virtuosity aside, it seems that what remains in them is a pilgrim wandering, almost groping his way, through a vast space, through a void. The 'Lugubrious Gondola' no longer recalls Venice at all. Instead, it reminds me of a few pages of Leopardi, like 'A se stesso' (To Himself), in which, exhausted, he reaches the depths of despair.

Always the same grove of very tall plane trees, taller every year, the colour of fire, lifting their highest branches to the level of the blue mountain ridges. I think of a dress such as Klimt painted except that it breathes better, an aerated, openwork dress—in any case a royal spectacle at this hour, at this time of year. 'Head of gold.' This noble bearing allows for no pettiness. A vegetal castle? They are fed by a stream, La Chalerne, more often stagnant than leaping or loquacious. And it's as if they raised to the highest degree the mirroring of the water running at their feet after having skirted the covered playground and the children's voices.

All the metamorphoses of movement, of time. And so we think we are slowing the course of our lives by writing words on leaves that the slightest puff of wind can disperse.

That we experience nausea more and more often at the sight of the world could take away some of the conviction to write we have left; or, on the contrary, it might give us one more reason to preserve, to show the valley that on a previous day opened up, expanded to receive the afternoon light into its conch shell. We saw the grass gleaming at the foot of the flame-coloured trees. Final warmth of the year, most tangible to those leaving.

Listened again to Webern who reminds me of Morandi, at least in his extreme concentration, his extreme economy of means. In a letter to Alban Berg in August 1919, he writes of his love for mountains:

> . . . the search for what is highest . . . The cause of my emotion: that profound, unfath-omable, inexhaustible meaning we find in all of nature's manifestations . . . I've discovered a plant: the 'wintergreen' [In fact, it is pyrola, in the ericaceae family]. A small plant like the lily-of-the-valley, invisible, difficult to detect. But that balsamic fragrance. What a fragrance! For me it is the quintessence

of tenderness, of movement, of depth, of
purity . . .

On 14 February 1945, his only son Peter died in an
aerial bombing attack on a train. He himself, fleeing
Vienna with his wife, was killed by mistake by a
drunken American soldier. His wife died four years
later.

DECEMBER

Joubert's *Notebooks*. I would like to quote all his youth-
ful prose, of 1787, perhaps, titled 'Night Musicians':

> Those musicians who walk about in small
> groups also move around the city during the
> day. Occasionally, in summer, one is tempted
> to believe in the city of Baghdad as described
> in *A Thousand and One Nights*, in which the
> streets were sprinkled with perfumed water
> and the houses echoed with cheerful song.
> The bouquets that are piled up at crossings
> and that perfume the air, the strolling musi-
> cians, performing here and there, and crowds
> of honest people at their windows; all this
> together has at times an inexpressible charm.

The beginning of this prose, which I did not quote, could have been written by Leopardi: on the power of music heard from a distance in the silence of night. Joubert was born in 1754. Leopardi came into the world a few decades later. In every era, there is probably a network of minds very close to one another, even if they are most often unaware of one another: marvellous constellations we like to discover in our own skies.

If I were to indulge, I'd quote page after page. But these few words suspended in the air: 'Snows—when the curtain has been raised . . . ' should be included in my personal alchemical repertory of phrases that have served as Open Sesames for a long time, their power still undiminished despite the passing years. Another note of 25 January 1802 answers that note on the same theme: 'The white traces of snow, scattered here and there on the greenery in times of thaw.'

An intuition from July 1806: 'Scents are like the souls of flowers. They can be sensed even in the country of shadows.' And this brief note: 'A dove. Bitter seeds and clear water' . . . What did he mean? He shines a strange light on these few words.

This, too, could serve as a rule: 'It is better to be concerned with being than with nothingness. Consider then what you still have rather than what you have lost.' A golden rule, in truth.

Got up a bit earlier than usual this morning (seven o'clock). On opening the kitchen shutters onto the garden, Venus' brilliance was like a trumpet blast, a cry of joy to bring walls tumbling down.

An entire herd of hills in their fleece, their fur of trees; the way we dominate them with our gaze, we would gladly think ourselves their shepherd. And yet, the twilight inflames or empurples the higher mountains in the distance, it gilds the surface of the rocks as a bright half-moon appears and scattered clouds sit like smoke over a few shadowy slopes. These brief fires of the mountains in graceful and fresh company: How can one say 'everything is bad'?

A beautiful film of Shakespeare's *Henry V* made by Kenneth Branagh, thanks mostly to his interpretation and the mastery with which he recreates the Battle of Agincourt. At first, I had told myself that the kind of heroic speech Shakespeare delivers in the play, celebrating the young king's bravery and greatness, could hardly be heard today. Then we were shown images of the war in Chechnya: the slow progression of Russian tanks seemed to me extraordinarily close to that of the armoured horse heads advancing on the exhausted, badly supplied English soldiers. These, in turn, seemed closed to those wretches in wool hats preparing Molotov cocktails, to the armed women screaming their willingness to fight, and to that lunatic dancing with a drawn sabre to give himself a bit of fire in the belly: a real person, terrifying, whom a theatre critic would probably deem excessive on a Shakespearean stage. Here we have stories as old as the world, never ceasing resuming and spreading destruction, enough to despair.

In the middle of the night, which encourages concentration and even a certain exaltation by erasing the world, I thought again of those mountains as I saw them on our recent walks and I told myself, probably in a vaguely feverish moment, that from now on I should capture that radiance 'as is' in words. What I meant by that: shorn of all connection to my life, my desires, dreams or fears; as if I could strip them of a kind of coat and mask and show them in the calm radiance of their reality like things almost absolute—as well as, moreover, realities that are more modest, more frail, like the wild clematis that invades, like dirty flakes of snow, a very old orchard near a ruin on a hillside while the rain digs muddy ruts in the roads. It was as if, in this state of half-waking, I felt their existence, their presence with more immediacy, more intensity than ever before, indisputable; and as if nothing could take this gift from me—one I received in a way that was all the more pure for not having been magnetized by any passion. But other presences were also a part of this radiant reality: the child at play, the women—young or less young, the men we were— living like clouds caught in the leafless forests or those that would be set alight later in that part of the sky that was still yellow at sunset. And yet, also present, to the same degree, the immanent shadow, heavy with cold and night, the moon cut in two, a stocky horse, its white coat dirtied with mud, escaped from its pen— and the words exchanged like an invisible pattern.

In Shentalinsky's book, *Arrested Voices*, devoted to the KGB files on writers who disappeared under Stalinism, there is the written testimony of a certain Ivan Okunev, arrested in 1938 when he was twenty and, like Shalamov, deported to a camp in Kolyma, which surpasses in horror everything I've read on the subject. As the author writes: 'There! That is all and that's enough. After this there is nothing else today about the prisons and the camps. How could one say more than this simple account, this breath, these simple words exhaled by one simple, unknown man.'[53]

It's impossible to know if the pages on Mandelstam's end in his camp, hardly any less gruelling, conform completely to the truth of events. The likelihood, unfortunately, is very great.

To touch up what I wrote in January, having ingested a bit too many of Ronsard's poems in succession: first, in order to avoid this reaction it's necessary to disregard those notes in which the recollection of supposed ancient sources for a number of verses aggravates the impression that there is only bookish writing in this work; then one must choose pages at random, the way people used to look for advice or predictions in random verses from the Bible. Then, the odds are great that you will once again be enchanted by this supreme art of verbal construction when a more natural inflection, like a caress, changes marble into desirable flesh:

> I would wash her body and call blessed
> This water become my beautiful beloved . . .

or

> Love's ardour like straw set alight . . .

or in a critique of the artificiality of life in court— a traditional critique that can be found in a more

developed form in one of Góngora's *Solitudes*—a line
in which we think we can already hear Nerval:

Your Circe, your Siren and your sorceress . . .

It occurs to me that you could collect all kinds of 'pass-
words' taken from any particular time and place—like
the fragment of Hölderlin's hymn 'Columbus', which
was, not by chance, as important to André du Bouchet
(' . . . discordant as if by snow . . . ') as it was to me, or
this or that haiku I have quoted, as well as this or that
poem or group of poems by Baudelaire or Leopardi—
and set them against the 'formulas' enunciated in the
thinking of philosophers that, however profound or
persuasive, have never allowed me to glimpse the
openings that these few lyrical blazes have offered me.

A television documentary on the 'mountain sculptors'
in China, in the south of the Yunnan Province. Moun-
tains completely altered by man, transformed into ter-
races for growing rice, terraces amply irrigated by
mountain streams. Seen from above and at a distance,
the landscape resembles those enamel objects in fash-
ion at the time in the modern style, if I'm not mis-
taken: mirroring an undulant geometry in which the
earth is nothing more than the water's border.

A return in time of several centuries, about which you must admit, even if reluctantly, that it could feed a fit of backward-looking nostalgia. It does seem that everything there is still 'beautiful': the women's clothing, black adorned with dark blues or bright reds, the sorcerers' or scholars' pipes that are as large as bass flutes and sound like narghiles when they inhale, the millstones for grinding rice, the gestures made by the 'guardian of the water' before opening the sluice for the mountain streams to fill the new terraces, those of the 'great dragon' walking through the village lanes to chase the spirits away, a knife in each hand and followed by chanting children in costume—all of it including the gait of the ploughing bull and the great lyre of its striate horns.

Even so, should we then think that a 'truth' superior to ours reigns there?

They have been filmed: it's the beginning of the end of their seclusion.

The parable in Attar's *Book of Affliction* is worth remembering:

> A destitute old woman, turned white by the
> years, was standing at the cemetery gate. On
> a strip of cloth she held in her hands, she had

sewn more than a thousand dots. Each time a dead person was brought to the cemetery, she added one. Whether one or ten bodies were brought, she made a mark for each of the dead. Because deaths occurred constantly, the rag was covered with millions of dots.

One day, death cut such a swathe that it ruined the old woman's business. So many corpses were brought at once, she lost track. Overwhelmed, she gave a cry, cut the thread and broke the needle! 'I have no use for this work!' she exclaimed. 'How long will I be here with a thread and needle in hand? From now on, I won't use the needle any more and I'll throw this rag in the fire! This question has been bothering me non-stop. How will I get an answer from a needle and a piece of thread? May I be granted passionate whirling like the celestial sphere! This is not a matter of needle and thread!'

The words will never reach your ear, oblivious and shallow as you are! For if you heard a single one of these words, the shirt on your back would become a shroud!

This is not a matter of needle and thread! . . .

First, the image of this old woman sewing at the graveyard gate, then the image of the rag covered with dots spoke to me. That is to say, the image of a daily task, like another, very beautiful one in one of Ronsard's most justifiably famous sonnets:

> Then not one of your serving girls on hearing
> those words
> Though half asleep over her needle work . . .

A task we seem to remember having seen on a distant childhood evening, independent of the meaning Attar would give it.

I'm not sure if I'm seriously misrepresenting this parable—ignorant as I am about ancient Persian thought—by imagining what it might have to say to us today: that the fear of death, the horror of millions and millions of dead accumulating since the beginning of history, is not simply a matter of accounting, which would soon wear away even the most patient fingers, wear down the most valiant soul, and for which even a cloth as large as the universe would not suffice. Yet the only response to give is the sacred dance that corresponds to the silent revolutions of the night sky; or, for the rest of us, more modestly, since we no longer dance like dervishes, the attempt to catch the sound of the world and translate it onto the fabric of the page, which none would then think of seeing as a shroud.

NOTES

1 Jacques Masui, *Cheminements* [Wanderings] (Paris: Fayard, 1978).

2 Farid ud-Din Attar, *The Conference of Birds* [*c*.1177] (Afkham Darbandi and Dick Davis trans) (London: Penguin, 1984).

3 Gerard Manley Hopkins, 'Binsey Poplars' in *Poems* (Robert Bridges ed. and annot.) (London: Humphrey Milford, 1918). Available at: https://goo.gl/SxJs6D (last accessed on 10 June 2017).

4 Hopkins, 'Moonrise' in *Poems*. Available at: https://goo.gl/yfR6Ch (last accessed on 8 July 2017).

5 Hopkins, 'Spring' in *Poems*. Available at: https://goo.gl/rWB3gB (last accessed on 8 July 2017).

6 Virgina Woolf, *Orlando*: *A Biography* (London: Hogarth Press, 1928).

7 Dante Alighieri, *The Paradiso* (Geoffrey L. Bickersteth trans.) (Cambridge: Cambridge University Press, 1932). Jaccottet quotes André Pézard's 1965 French translation: 'Leur vol ardent les lie au point, qui'ils suivent / de plus près, pour lui être au mieux semblables; / et plus haute est leur vue, plus lui ressemblent.'

8 Hopkins, 'Inversnaid' in *Poems*. Available at: https://goo.gl/iGgQEz (last accessed on 8 July 2017).

9 Hopkins, 'Patience, hard thing! the hard thing but to pray' in *Poems*. Available at: https://goo.gl/JKS5o7 (last accessed on 8 July 2017).

10 James McNeil Whistler, *Ten O'Clock: A Lecture* (Portland, ME: T. B. Mosher, 1916). Available at: https://goo.gl/-3pRC45 (last accessed on 8 July 2017). The lecture was actually delivered on 20 February 1885.

11 Henri Michaux, *Poteaux D'Angle* [Corner Posts] (Paris: Gallimard, 1981).

12 André Dhôtel, *Rhétorique fabuleuse* [Fabulous Rhetoric] (Paris: Garnier, 1983).

13 Jean Paulhan, *Le Clair et l'obscur: Actes du colloque de Cerisy-la-Salle 1998* [The Clear and the Obscure: Proceedings of the Cerisy-la-Salle Symposium, 1998] (Paris: Gallimard, 1999).

14 Henri Thomas, *Le migrateur* [The Migrant] (Paris: Gallimard, 1983).

15 Mircea Eliade, *Myth and Reality* (Willard R. Trask trans.) (New York: Harper and Row, 1963), p. 141. Although the first chapter of the book is titled 'The Structure of Myths', the quoted lines are to be found in the eighth chapter, 'Greatness and Decadence of Myths'.

16 Emily Brönte, 'Fall, Leaves, Fall' in J. C. Squire (ed.), *A Book of Women's Verse* (Oxford: Clarendon, 1921). Jaccottet quotes from the French translation, Emily Jane Brönte, *Poémes, 1836–1846* (Pierre Leyris trans.) (Paris: Gallimard, 1963): 'Tombez, feuilles, tomez; et vous, fleurs, périssez! / Que s'allonge la nuit, que s'abrège le jour! / Toute feuille me parle de félicité / Qui tournoie, détachée de la branche d'automne / Je sourirai lorsque la neige et ses guirlandes / Fleuriront où devrait encore croître la rose; / Je chanterai quand la nuit déclinante / Sera l'huissier d'un jour plus désolé.'

17 Jorge Luis Borges, *Labyrinths* (James E. Irby trans.) (New York: New Directions, 1964), p. 188.

18 Jorge Luis Borges, 'Rain' (Alastair Reid trans.) in *Selected Poems* (Alexander Coleman ed.) (London: Penguin, 1999), p. 115.

19 Emily Dickinson, 'Where Every Bird Is Bold to Go' in *The Complete Poems of Emily Dickinson* (Martha Dickinson Bianchi introd.) (Boston, MA: Little, Brown, 1924).

20 F. W. J. Schelling, *Clara; or, On Nature's Connection to the Spirit World* (Fiona Steinkamp ed. and introd.) (New York: State University of New York Press, 2002), p. 13. Subsequent quotes are from the same edition, pp. 15, 32, 46, 63.

21 Rainer Maria Rilke, 'Ninth Elegy' in *Duino Elegies* (J. B. Lieshman and Stephen Spender trans) (London: Hogarth Press, 1939), pp. 149–52.

22 Peter Handke, *Absence* (Ralph Manheim trans.) (New York: Farrar, Straus and Giroux, 1990), pp. 43–4.

23 Actually Paul Celan was born in 1920; so he was 68 in 1988.

24 Johann Wolfgang von Goethe, 'Autumn 1775' (Robert M. Browning trans.) in Robert M. Browning (ed.), *German Poetry from 1750 to 1900* (London: Bloomsbury Academic, 1984): 'Green more greenly, you leaves / On the grape-vined wall, / Upwards here to my window. / Tighten your skins tighter still, / Twinned clusters, ripen faster / And lustrously fuller. / Brooding rays of Mother Sun's / Parting glance warms you, 'Kind heaven's fructifying fullness / Whispers about you, / The friendly moon's magic breath / Cools you, and, O, / From these eyes / Ever animating love's / Full swelling tears bedew you.'

25 François-René de Chateaubriand, *Mémoires d'Outre-Tombe* (Paris: Penaud frères, 1849–50). Available in English translation as: *Memoirs from Beyond the Tomb* (Robert Baldick trans.) (London: Penguin Classics, 2014).

26 Angelus Silenius, *Pélerine Chérubinique* (Roger Munier trans.) (Paris: Arfuyen, 1988).

27 Buson, *Haïku* (Nobuko Imamura and Alain Gouvret trans.) (Paris: Arfuyen, 1988).

28 This and following quotes from: Dante Alighieri, *Vita Nuova* (Mark Musa trans.) (Oxford: Oxford University Press, 2008), pp. 15, 35, 80, 81.

29 Jean-Michel Frank, *Musique, raison ardente* [Music, Ardent Reason] (Paris: Obsidiane, 1983).

30 Dante Alighieri, *Selected Rime* (A. S. Kline trans.). Available at: https://goo.gl/6dnfrt (last accessed on 11 July 2017).

31 W. B. Yeats, 'Memory' in *The Collected Poems of W. B. Yeats* (London: Wordsworth Poetry Library, 2000), p. 125. In French: '*Quarante-cinq poèmes*' *suivi de* '*La Résurrection*' (Yves Bonnefoy trans.) (Paris: Gallimard, 1993).

32 Johann Wolfgang von Goethe, 'Alexis und Dora' in *Goethes Werke*, Hamburg Edition, VOL. 1 (Munich: C. H. Beck, 1998). Available at: https://goo.gl/LifhRc (last accessed on 12 July 2017).

33 Henri Thomas, *Le Monde absent* (Paris: Gallimard, 1947).

34 John Keats, 'Letter to James Rice, 16 February 1820' in *The Letters of John Keats*, *Volume 2, 1819–1821* (Hyder Edward Rollins ed.) (Cambridge: Cambridge University Press, 1958), p. 260. [Although Jaccottet states that the letter was written on 18 February, it is in fact dated 16 February 1820.]

35 Koyabashi Issa, *Die letzten Tage meines Vaters* [The Diary of My Father's Last Days] (G. S. Dombrady trans.) (Mainz: Dieterich'Sche Verlag, 1985).

36 Basho, *La Sente étroite du bout du monde* [The Narrow Road to the Ends of the Earth] (René Sieffert trans.) (Paris: Publications orientalistes de France, 1976).

37 Michel Leiris, *A Cor et à cri* [With Hue and Cry] (Paris: Gallimard, 1988).

38 Johann Wolfgang von Goethe, *Aus meinem Leben. Dichtung und Wahrheit* [From my Life: Poetry and Truth] (Berlin: Holzinger, 2016). English translation available from Project Gutenberg at: https://goo.gl/8WcSGw (last accessed on 11 July 2017).

39 Lev Shestov, *Athens and Jerusalem* (Bernard Marin trans. and introd.) (Athens: Ohio University Press, 1966), p. 363.

40 Friedrich Schiller, *On the Aesthetic Education of Man* (Reginald Snell trans. and introd.) (New Haven, CT: Yale University Press, 1954), p. 37.

41 Henri Thomas, *La Joie de cette vie* [The Joy of This Life] (Paris: Gallimard, 1991).

42 Louis-Ferdinand Céline, *Journey to the End of the Night* (Ralph Manheim trans.) (New York: New Directions, 2006[1983]), p. 256.

43 Eugenio Montale, 'Lindau' in *Collected Poems, 1920–1954* (Jonathan Galassi trans.) (New York: Farrar, Strauss and Giroux, 1998).

44 Ezra Pound and Ernest Fellonosa, *The Classic Noh Theatre of Japan* (New York: New Directions, 1959), pp. 76–88.

45 Johann Wolfgang von Goethe, *Die Wahlverwandtschaften* [Elective Affinities] (Berlin: J. G. Cottaische Buchhandlung, 1809). Available in English translation as: *Elective Affinities* (R. J. Hollingdale trans.) (London: Penguin, 1971).

46 Edgar Morin, *L'Esprit du temps* [The Spirit of the Times] (Paris: Grasset, 1962).

47 Paul de Roux's *La Halte obscure: Poèmes* [The Obscure Stop: Poems] (Paris: Gallimard, 1993).

48 Tomas Tranströmer, 'Schubertiana' in *The Great Enigma: New Collected Poems* (Robin Fulton trans.) (New York: New Directions, 2006), p. 148.

49 Makoto Ooka (ed.), *Poèmes de tous les jours* (Everyday Poems) (Yves Marie Allios trans.) (Paris: Éditions Philippe Picquier, 1999).

50 Plato, *The Republic* (Benjamin Jowett trans.). Available at: https://goo.gl/tQ5ZgW (last accessed on 12 July 2017).

51 José Angel Valente, *Landscape with Yellow Birds* (Tom Christensen trans.) (New York: Archipelago Books, 2013), pp. 257, 259, 295.

51 'Each brilliant day, each blooming hill I see, whatever I enjoy, I say / Nerina enjoys nothing now. She doesn't see the fields, the air . . . ' Giacomo Leopardi, *Canti*: *Poems* (Jonathan Galassi trans.) (New York: Farrar, Straus and Giroux, 2011), p. 16.

52 Vitaly Shentalinsky, *Arrested Voices*: *Resurrecting the Disappeared Writers of the Soviet Regime* (John Crowfoot trans.) (New York: Free Press, 1996).